Louis Althusser

Verso

Montesquieu, Rousseau, Marx

Politics and History

Translated from the French by Ben Brewster

'Montesquieu: Politics and History' first published
by Presses Universitaires de France, Paris, 1959,
© PUF, 1959; 'The Social Contract' first published in
Cahiers pour l'Analyse, no. 8: *L'Impensé de Jean-
Jacques Rousseau*, n.d., © Le Graphe; 'Marx's Relation
to Hegel' first published in *Hegel et la Pensée
Moderne* by Presses Universitaires de France, Paris, 1970,
© PUF, 1970.

This translation first published, 1972
© NLB, 1972

Verso edition 1982

Verso Editions/NLB, 15 Greek Street, London W1

Designed by Gerald Cinamon
Typeset in Monotype Ehrhardt
and printed by
Butler and Tanner Ltd, Frome, Somerset

Acknowledgments: We are grateful to J. M. Dent & Sons Ltd for their kind permission to use extracts from *The Social Contract and Discourses*, translated by G. D. H. Cole, and from *Émile*, translated by Barbara Foxley, both published in Everyman's Library.

Translator's note: Quotations from the works of Montesquieu in Part One of this book have in general been taken from the four-volume translation by Thomas Nugent entitled *The Works of Monsieur de Montesquieu*, published in London in 1777. References to the *Spirit of Laws* give the Book number in Roman and the chapter number in Arabic numerals: thus, SL, VIII, 9 means *The Spirit of Laws*, Book VIII, Chapter 9. Quotations from Rousseau in Parts One and Two have been taken either from *The Social Contract and Discourses*, translated by G. D. H. Cole, in the Everyman's Library edition of 1966, or from *Émile*, translated by Barbara Foxley, in the Everyman's Library edition of 1957. Page references are to these editions. However, the translator has taken the liberty of altering these translations whenever questions of consistency of terminology, or facilitating the reader's understanding of Althusser's commentary, have arisen. Quotations from Marx, Engels and Lenin in Part Three have been taken from the standard English translations of their works, published in England by Lawrence and Wishart.

Part One

Montesquieu:
Politics and History

To apply the ideas of the present time to distant ages,
is the most fruitful source of error. To those
people who want to modernize all the ancient ages,
I shall say what the Egyptian priests said to
Solon, 'O Athenians, you are mere children.'
The Spirit of Laws, xxx, 14.

Montesquieu made us see . . .   Mme De Staël

France had lost her claims to nobility; Montesquieu
gave her them back.   Voltaire

Foreword

I make no claim to say anything new about Montesquieu. Anything that seems to be new is no more than a reflection on a well-known text or on a pre-existing reflection.

I simply hope that I have given a more living portrait of a figure familiar to us in marble or bronze. I am not thinking so much of the inner life of the Seigneur de la Brède, which was so secret that it is still debated whether he was ever a believer, whether he loved his wife as she loved him, whether past the age of thirty-five he experienced the passions of a twenty-year-old. Nor so much the everyday life of the Président de Parlement tired of parliament, of the lord absorbed by his lands, of the vineyardist attentive to his wines and his sales. Others have written of this, and they should be read. I am thinking of a different life, one which time has cloaked in its shadow, and commentaries with their lustre.

This life is, first, that of a thinker whose enthusiasm in legal and political matters never waned to the end, and who spoilt his sight by too much reading, hurrying to win the only race with death that really concerned him, his completed work. But let there be no misunderstanding: it is not the *curiosity* of his object, but his *intelligence*, which is all Montesquieu. His only wish was to *understand*. We have several images of him which betray this effort and his pride in it. He only delved into the infinite mass of documents and texts, the immense heritage of histories, chronicles miscellanies and compilations, in order to grasp their logic and disengage their grounds. He wanted to seize the 'thread' of this skein which centuries had tangled, to seize this thread and pull it to him so that the whole followed. The whole did follow. At other times he felt himself lost in this gigantic universe of minute data as if in a boundless sea. He wanted this sea to have shores, he wanted to give it them and reach them. He reached them. No one went before him in this adventure. It is as if this man, who was enough in love with ships to discuss the design of their hulls, the height of their masts and their speeds; who devoted enough interest to the first *peripli* to follow the Carthaginians down the coasts of Africa and the Spaniards to India, felt some affinity with all sea-rovers. Not in vain does he invoke the sea when he finds himself in the wide open spaces of his subject: the last sentence of his book celebrates the longed-for approach to land. It is true that he set out for the unknown. But for this navigator, too, the unknown was simply a new land.

That is why Montesquieu reveals something of the profound joy of a man who *discovers*. He knows it. He knows he is bringing new ideas, that he is offering a work without precedent, and if his last words are a salute to the land finally conquered, his first is to warn that he set out alone and had no teachers; nor did his thought have a mother. He notes that he really must use a new language because he is speaking new truths. Even his turns of phrase betray the pride of an author who illuminates the ordinary words he has inherited with the new meanings he has discovered. In that moment when he is almost surprised to see its birth and is seized by it, and in the thirty years of labour which constituted his career, he is well aware that his thought opens up a *new world*. We have got used to this discovery. And when we celebrate its greatness, we cannot but let Montesquieu be already fixed in the necessity of our culture, as a star is in the sky, perceiving only with difficulty the audacity and enthusiasm he must have had to open to us this sky in which we have inscribed him.

But I am also thinking of another life. Of the life too often masked by the very same discoveries that we owe to him. Of his preferences, his aversions, in short, of Montesquieu's *parti pris* in the struggles of his age. A too soothing tradition would like Montesquieu to have cast on the world the gaze of a man without interest or party. Did he not himself say that he was a historian precisely because he was detached from every faction, shielded from power and all its temptations, free of everything by a miraculous chance? Capable precisely of understanding because free of everything? Let us do him the duty, which is the duty of every historian, of taking him not at his word, but at his work. It has seemed to me that this image is a myth, and I hope to show it. But in showing it I should not like anyone to believe that Montesquieu's enthusiastic *parti pris* in the political struggles of his time ever reduced his work to a mere commentary on his wishes.

Others before him set out for the East – and discovered Indies for us in the West.

Chapter One

A Revolution in Method

It is a received truth that Montesquieu is the *founder of political science*. Auguste Comte said it, Durkheim repeated it and no one has seriously disputed their judgement. But perhaps we should step back a little in order to distinguish him from his ancestors, and to see clearly into what it is that thus distinguishes him.

For even Plato stated that politics is the object of a science, and we have his *Republic*, *Politics* and *Laws* to prove it. All of the thought of antiquity lived in the conviction, not that a science of politics was possible, which is a critical conviction, but that one could go ahead with it straight away. And the moderns themselves took up this thesis, as is clear from Bodin, Hobbes, Spinoza and Grotius. Of course, the Ancients should be criticized not for their claim to reflect on the political, but for their illusory belief that they had produced a *science* of it. For their idea of science was borrowed from their own knowledges. And as the latter, with the exception of certain areas of mathematics, not unified before Euclid, were no more than immediate glimpses or their philosophy projected into things, they were complete strangers to our idea of science, having no examples of it. But the Moderns! How could the mind of a Bodin, of a Machiavelli, of a Hobbes or of a Spinoza, the contemporaries of the already rigorous disciplines triumphing in mathematics and physics, have remained blind to the model of scientific knowledge that we have inherited?

And in fact from the sixteenth century on we can see the birth and growth in a joint movement of a first, mathematical physics, and of the demand for a second, soon to be called *moral* or *political physics*, which aimed for the rigour of the first. For the opposition between the sciences of nature and the sciences of man was not yet in season. The most metaphysical exiled into God this science of politics or history, which seemed to be the conjunction of the chances of fortune and the decrees of human freedom: Leibniz, for example. But all that is ever handed over to God is the errors of man – and Leibniz entrusted to God the human idea of a science of man. As for the positives, the moralists, the philosophers of law, the politicals, and Spinoza himself, they did not doubt for a moment that it was possible to treat human relations like physical relations. Hobbes only saw one difference between mathematics and the social sciences: the former unites men, the latter divide them. But that is only because in the former *the truth and men's interests are not opposed*, whereas in the latter *whenever reason goes against man, man is opposed to reason*. Spinoza, too, intended that human relations should be treated in the same way as natural things, and by the same routes. For example, take the pages that introduce the *Political Treatise*: Spinoza denounces the pure philosophers who, as the Aristotelians do with nature, project into politics the imaginary of their concepts or ideals, and he proposes to replace their dreams with the real science of history. How then can we claim that Montesquieu opened routes which we find completely mapped out well before him?

In fact, if he seems to follow known routes, he is not going to the same *objects*. Helvétius says of Montesquieu that he has Montaigne's 'cast of mind'. He has the same curiosity and takes the same matter for reflection. Like Montaigne and all his disciples, collectors of examples and facts hunted out from every place and time, he takes as his object *the entire history of all the men who have ever lived*. And this idea did not come to him altogether by chance. We must imagine the double revolution that shook the world at the turn of the fifteenth and sixteenth centuries. A revolution in its space. A revolution in its structure. It is the age of the discovery of the Earth, of the great explorations opening up to Europe the knowledge and the exploitation of the Indies East and West and of Africa. Travellers brought back in their coffers spices and gold, and in their memories the tale of customs and institutions which overthrew all the received truths. But this scandal would have had the impact of a mere curiosity had it not been for the fact that in the very heart of the countries which were thus sending forth their ships for the conquest of the new lands, other events, too, were shaking the foundations of these convictions. Civil wars, the religious revolution of the Reformation, wars of religion, the transformation of the traditional structure of the State, the rise of the commoners, the humbling of the great – these upheavals, whose echo can be heard in all the works of the period, gave the material of the scandalous tales brought back from across the seas the contagious dignity of facts real and full of meaning. What had previously been themes for compilation, extravaganzas to appease the passions of the erudite, became a kind of mirror for the contemporary unease and the fantastic echo of this world in crisis. This is the basis for the *political exoticism* (known history itself, Greece and Rome, becoming the *other world* in which the present world seeks its own image) which has dominated thought since the sixteenth century.

Such is Montesquieu's object, too. As he says, 'The objects of this work are the Laws, the various customs, and manners, of all the nations on earth. It may be said, that the subject is of prodigious extent, as it comprehends all the institutions received among mankind.'[1] It is precisely this object that distinguishes him from all the writers who, before him, had hoped to make politics a science. For never before him had anyone had the daring to reflect on *all the customs and laws of all the nations of the world*. Bossuet's history does claim to be universal: but all its universality consists of is the statement that the Bible says everything, all of history being in it, as an oak is in its acorn. As for theoreticians like Hobbes, Spinoza or Grotius, they *propose* the idea of a science of history rather than *working it out*. They reflect not on the totality of concrete facts but either on some of them (Spinoza on the Jewish State and its ideology in the

1. *A Defence of the Spirit of Laws*, Part II: The General Idea.

Theologico-Political Treatise), or on *society in general* (Hobbes in *De Cive* and *Leviathan*, Spinoza himself in the *Political Treatise*). They do not produce a theory of real history, but a theory of the essence of society. They do not explain any particular society, nor any concrete historical period, nor *a fortiori* all societies and all history. They analyse the essence of society and provide an ideal and abstract model of it. We might say that their science is as far from Montesquieu's as the speculative physics of a Descartes is from the experimental physics of a Newton. The one directly attains in simple natures or essences the *a priori truth* of all possible physical facts, the other starts from the facts, observing their variations in order to disengage their *laws*. This difference in objects then governs a revolution in method. If Montesquieu was not the first to conceive of the idea of a social physics, he was the first to attempt to give it the spirit of the new physics, to set out not from essences but from facts, and from these facts to disengage their laws.

Hence it is clear both what unites Montesquieu with the theoreticians who preceded him and what distinguishes him from them. He has in common with them *the same project*: to erect a political science. But *he does not have the same object*, proposing to produce the science not of society in general but of all the concrete societies in history. And for this reason *he does not have the same method*, aiming not to grasp essences, but to discover laws. This unity in project and difference in object and method make Montesquieu both the man who gave his predecessors' *scientific exigencies* the most rigorous form – and the most determined opponent of their *abstraction*.

The project of constituting a science of politics and history presupposes first of all that politics and history can be the object of a science, i.e. that they contain a *necessity* which the science can hope to discover. It is therefore necessary to overthrow the sceptical idea that the history of humanity is no more than the history of its errors and divagations; that a single principle can unite the prodigious and daunting diversity of manners and morals: man's weakness; that a single reason can illuminate that infinite disorder: man's very unreason. It is necessary to say, 'I have first of all considered mankind; and the result of my thoughts has been, that, amidst such an infinite diversity of laws and manners, they were not solely conducted by the caprice of fancy' (SL, Preface), but by a deeper reason, which, if not always reasonable, is at least always rational; by a necessity whose empire is so strict that it embraces not only bizarre institutions, which last, but even the accident that produces victory or defeat in a battle and is contained in a momentary encounter.[2] This rational necessity rejects, along with the scepticism which is its pretext, all the temptations of Pascal's apologetics, espying in human unreason the admission of a divine reason; and all recourse to principles which surpass man in man, like religion, or assign him ends, like morality. In order to begin to be scientific, the necessity which governs history must stop borrowing its reasons from any order transcending history. It must therefore clear from the way of science the pretensions of a *theology* and a *morality* which would like to dictate it their own laws.

It is not for *theology* to pronounce on the truth of the facts of politics. An old argument. But it is hard to imagine today the weight of ecclesiastical decree on history. It is enough to read Bossuet's campaign against Spinoza, guilty of having outlined a history of the Jewish nation and the Bible, or against Richard Simon, who had the same project inside the Church itself, to see the conflict between theology and history, and its violence. This conflict occupies the whole of the *Defence of the Spirit of Laws*. Montesquieu was accused of atheism, of deism; of not having mentioned original sin; of having condoned polygamy, etc.; in short, of having reduced laws to purely human causes. Montesquieu replies: to introduce theology into history is to confuse orders and mix up sciences, which is the surest way to keep them in their childhood. No, his aim is not to play the theologian; he is not a theologian but a jurist and a politician. That all the objects of political science may have a religious meaning, *too*, that

2. SL, X, 13 (the battle of Pultova); *Considerations on the Causes of the Grandeur and Declension of the Roman Empire*, Ch. XVIII.

celibacy, polygamy and usury can be decided on theologically, he would agree. But all these facts derive also and first from an order foreign to theology, from an autonomous order which has its own principles. Let them therefore leave him in peace. He does not forbid anyone to judge *as a theologian*. Let them therefore grant him in exchange the right to judge as a *politician*. And let them not go seek theology in his politics. There is no more theology in his politics than there is a steeple in the telescope through which the curate was shown the moon.[3]

Thus religion cannot stand in for science in history. Nor can *morality*. Montesquieu takes the utmost care at the outset to warn against understanding *morality* when he says *politics*. The same for *virtue*. 'It is not a moral, nor a Christian, but a political virtue' (SL, Advertisement). And if he returns a dozen times to this warning, it is because here he runs up against the commonest prejudice: 'in all countries morality is requisite' (ibid.). Hobbes and Spinoza said the same thing: all the duties in the world do not constitute the beginning of a single *knowledge*; in his morality, which wants to make the man he is the man he is not, man only too obviously admits that the laws that govern him are not moral. Hence a determination to reject morality is essential if these laws are to be penetrated. Human and Christian virtues are held up against Montesquieu when he attempts to understand the scandalous usages of the Chinese and the Turks! 'It is not usual to crowd these questions into books of natural philosophy, politics and civil law.'[4] Here, too, distinct orders must be distinguished: 'All political are not moral vices; and all . . . moral are not political vices' (SL, XIX, 11). Each order having its own laws, it only lays claim to laws of its own. He replies to the theologians and moralists that he only wants to speak *humanely* of the human order of things, and politically of the political order. He defends his most profound conviction: that a science of politics can never be founded except on its own object, on the radical autonomy of the political as such.

3. *A Defence of the S L*, Part I, 11, Answer to the 9th Objection.
4. *A Defence of the S L*, Part II: On Climate.

But the cause is not yet understood. For it is not enough to distinguish the sciences and their orders: in life the orders overlap one another. True religion, true morality, supposing that they are excluded from the political order as explanatory principles, do nonetheless belong to that order by the conduct and scruples they inspire! Here the conflict becomes an acute one. For it is easy to render morality unto morality and to judge only as a pure politician. That is all right when one is writing about the horrifying morality of the Japanese or the terrifying religion of the Turks. All the theologians in the world will leave them to you. But when by chance one encounters the true morality! And the true religion! Can one treat them, too, 'humanely', as purely human things? Show that the *Christian* religion and morality, like those of the pagans, can be explained by the political regime, two degrees of latitude, an over harsh sky, the manners and morals of merchants and fishermen? Is it permissible to print that it is the difference in climate that has preserved Catholicism in the South of Europe and spread Protestantism in the North? Can one thus authorize *a political sociology of religion and morality*? The contagion of this evil imposes a return to its source, and the theologians are seen to be the victims of the fate accorded to Mahomet or the Chinese. For it is all right for *false* religions to be no more than human, and to fall beneath the profane empire of a science, but how can this empire be prevented from gaining the *true* religion? Hence the theologian who quickly scents the heresy in an over human theory of false religions. And Montesquieu who struggles and defends himself in the terribly narrow margin separating his convictions as a believer (or his dishonest precautions) from his exigencies as a scientist. For there is no doubt but that, on many occasions, Montesquieu expounds in his examples the complete argument of a true *sociological theory of religious and moral beliefs*: Religion and morality, which he correctly refuses the right to judge history, are no more than elements internal to given societies which govern their forms and their nature. The same principle that explains a given society also explains its beliefs. What, then, is left of the distinction of orders? The distinction, if it is to be maintained, and it has to be, traverses, then, the order of religion and morality itself. Religion can be said to be understood in its human meaning and role (which can fall within a sociology) or in its religious meaning (which falls outside any sociology). That is how Montesquieu retreats, in order to avoid jumping.

Hence the accusation of atheism, and the weakness of his defence. For if he gave his answers vigour, he could not give his arguments power. Someone tries to convict him of atheism. His only argument: would an atheist write that this world, which goes on its way and follows its laws alone, was created by *an intelligence*? Someone argues that his position amounts to Spinozism and natural religion. His only reply: natural religion is not atheism, and anyway, I do not profess natural religion. All these defensive stands could not deceive his opponents or allies. Besides, the best defence he presents of religion, the encomium he openly makes to it in the Second Part of the *Spirit of Laws*, is as much that of a cynic as that of a believer. Take the polemic against Bayle (SL, XXIV, 2 & 6). Bayle argued that religion is contrary to society (that is the meaning of the paradox about the atheists). Montesquieu counters that it is indispensable and profitable to society. But by doing so he remains within Bayle's principle: the social function, the social and political utility of religion. All his admiration amounts to is to show that the Christian religion, which lays claim only to heaven, is very well-suited to the earth. But all the 'politicals' used this language, and Machiavelli first of all. In this completely 'human' language, faith does not find its birth-right. Quite different arguments are required to win over a theologian!

However, these two principles preliminary to any political science: that it is impermissible to judge history by religious or moral criteria, that on the contrary it is essential to rank religion and morality among the facts of history and subordinate them to the same science, do not radically distinguish Montesquieu from his predecessors. When all is said and done, Hobbes and Spinoza spoke the same language, and were treated as atheists in the same way. Montesquieu is unique precisely in taking the opposite position to these theoreticians, although he was their heir, and opposing on one decisive point the *theories of natural law* of which they were for the most part the proponents.

Let me specify this point. In his book on political theory, Vaughan shows that all the political theorists of the seventeenth and eighteenth centuries were, *with the exception of Vico and Montesquieu*, theoreticians of the *social contract*.[5] What does this exception mean? In order to decide, we must make a rapid survey of the theory of natural law and of the social contract.

What unites the philosophers of natural law and of the social contract is the fact that they pose the same problem: *what is the origin of society?*, and solve it by the same means: *the state of nature and the social contract*. It may seem very strange today to pose such a *problem of origins* and to wonder how men, whose physical existence, even, always presupposes a minimum of social existence, could have moved from a *zero* state of society to organized social relations, and how they crossed this primordial and radical threshold. And yet it was the dominant problem of political reflection of the period, and if its form is strange, its logic is profound. To show the radical origin of society (we are reminded of Leibniz, wanting to pierce the 'radical origin of things'), men must be taken before society: in the emergent state. Rising from the earth like pumpkins, said Hobbes. Naked, said Rousseau. Stripped not only of all the instruments of art, but above all of all human bonds. And they must be grasped in a state which is a *negation of society*. This emergent state is the *state of nature*. Certainly, the various writers give this primordial state different characteristics. Hobbes and Spinoza see in it the reign of the state of war, the strong triumphant over the weak. Locke claims that the men there live in peace. Rousseau, in an absolute solitude. The different features of the state of nature sometimes suggest the reasons why men will have to leave it, at others the springs of the future social state and the ideal of human

5. C. E. Vaughan, *Studies in the History of Political Philosophy* (Manchester, 1939), vol. II, pp. 253ff.

relations. Paradoxically, this state, ignorant of all society, *contains and illustrates in advance the ideal of a society to be created*. It is the end of history that is inscribed in its origin. Thus the 'freedom' of the individual in Hobbes, Spinoza and Locke. Similarly, the equality and independence of man in Rousseau. But all these writers have in common the same concept and the same problem: the state of nature is no more than the origin of a society whose genesis they want to describe.

It is the *social contract* that ensures the transition from the negation of society to the existing society. Here again it may seem strange to imagine the establishment of a society as the effect of a general convention, as if every convention did not already presuppose an established society. But we must accept this problematic since it was held to be a necessary one, and only ask *what this contract means*, this contract which is not a mere legal artifice but the expression of a very profound rationale. To say that the society of men emerges from a contract is indeed to declare truly *human and artificial* the origin of all human institutions. It is to say that society is the effect neither of a *divine* institution nor of a *natural* order. It is therefore above all to reject an old idea of the foundation of the social order and to propose a new one. It is clear what opponents are implied by the theory of the contract. Not only the theoreticians of the divine origin of all society, who may serve many causes though most often that of the established order, but particularly the proponents of the 'natural' (and not artificial) character of society: those who believe human relations to be planned in advance in a *nature* which is no more than the projection of the existing social order, in a nature in which men are inscribed in advance in *orders and estates*. To say what is at stake in a word, the theory of the social contract in general overthrows the *conviction peculiar to the feudal order*, the belief in the 'natural' inequality of men, in the necessity of orders and estates. It substitutes a contract between *equals*, a work of human art, for what feudal theoreticians attributed to 'nature' and to man's *natural sociability*. It is *therefore* generally a fairly sure index of discrimination between tendencies to consider that *the doctrine of natural sociability or of the instinct of sociability designates a theory of feudal inspiration, and the doctrine of the social contract a theory of 'bourgeois' inspiration*, even when it is in the service of absolute monarchy (in Hobbes for example). Indeed, the idea that men are the authors of their society in a primordial pact, which is sometimes duplicated into a pact of (civil) association and a pact of (political) domination, is thus a revolutionary idea, echoing in pure theory the social and political conflicts of a world in genesis. This idea is both a protest against the old order and the programme for a new order. It deprives the established social order and all the political problems then in dispute of any recourse to 'nature' (at least to that inegalitarian 'nature'), denounces a fraud in it and bases the institutions its authors defend, including absolute monarchy in struggle against the feudal lords, on *human convention*. It thus gives men the power to reject the old institutions, to set up new ones and if need be to revoke or reform them by a new convention. In this theory of the state of nature and of the social contract, apparently pure speculation, we can see a social and political order that is falling, and men founding on ingenious principles the new order they hope to defend or erect.

But these features of *polemic and petition* so characteristic of the theory of natural law explain precisely its *abstraction and idealism*. I said above that these theoreticians were restricted to the model of a Cartesian physics which knew only *ideal essences*. And those who would like to judge Montesquieu by comparing him with Descartes, as has been done,[6] or Newton, reduce him to an immediate but abstract appearance. This model of physics is only an epistemological model here: its true arguments are partly external to it. If the theoreticians I am discussing do not take Montesquieu's *object*: to understand the infinite diversity of human institutions in all times and places, it is not simply because of the mere aberration of a method inspired by the Cartesian model of science, but also for motives of quite another

6. Gustave Lanson, 'L'influence de la philosophie cartésienne sur la littérature française', *Revue de métaphysique et de morale*, Année 4, 1896, pp. 517–50, especially pp. 540–6.

import. They did not have the idea of explaining the institutions of all the peoples of the world, but of combating an already established order or of justifying an order which was nascent or about to be born. They did not want to *understand all the facts* but to *found, i.e. to propose and justify, a new order*. That is why it would be aberrant to look in Hobbes or Spinoza for a real history of the fall of Rome or of the emergence of feudal law. They were not concerned with the *facts*. Rousseau was to say openly that it is essential to start by 'laying facts aside'.[7] They were only concerned with *right*, i.e. with what *ought to be*. The facts were for them only the matter for the exercise of this right, and in some sense the mere occasion and reflection of its existence. But here they remained in what must really be called a *polemical and ideological* posture. They made the side they took the very reason of history. And their principles, which they presented as science, were no more than values committed in the struggles of their time – values which they had *chosen*.

I do not say that all was in vain in this gigantic undertaking: its effects can be demonstrated, and they are considerable. But it is clear how far Montesquieu's proposals distance him from these perspectives, and in this distance his arguments are more clearly distinguishable. They are twofold, political and method-ological, both tightly linked. Let us reflect, then, on the absence of any social contract in Montesquieu. There is indeed a *state of nature* of which Book I of the *Spirit of Laws* gives us a very rapid glimpse, but no social contract. On the contrary, 'I have never heard anybody talk of the law of nations', says Montesquieu in the 94th Persian Letter, 'but he carefully begun with inquiring into the origin of society; which appears ridiculous to me. If men did not form themselves into societies, if they avoided and fled from each other, it would be right to ask the reason, and to inquire why they kept themselves separate: but they are born united to one another, a son is born near his father, and there he continues; here is society and the cause of it.' This says every-

7. *Discourse on the Origin of Inequality among Men*, in *The Social Contract and Discourses*, translated by G. D. H. Cole (London, 1966), p. 161.

thing. A condemnation of the problem of origins as absurd. Society always precedes itself. The only problem, if there must be one, though it is one never encountered, would be why there were some men without society. No contract. To explain society, a man and his son are all that is required. It is thus hardly surprising to find, in the rapid review of the state of nature in Book I, that a certain fourth law stands in for this absent contract: the *instinct of sociability*. Here is a first indication pointing the way to a judgement of Montesquieu as an opponent of the theory of natural law for reasons related to a *parti pris of the feudal type*. All the political theory of the *Spirit of Laws* will reinforce this conviction.

But this conscious rejection of the problem and of the concepts of the theory of natural law leads to a second indication, no longer of politics, but of *method*. Here undoubtedly stands revealed Montesquieu's radical novelty. Rejecting the theory of natural law and the contract, Montesquieu at the same time rejects *the philosophical implications of its problematic*: above all the *idealism* of its procedures. He is, at least in his deliberate consciousness, poles apart from judging the fact by the right and proposing in the guise of an ideal genesis an *end* for human societies. He only knows *facts*. If he refuses to judge *what is* by *what ought to be*, it is because he does not draw his principles from his 'prejudices, but from the nature of things' (SL, Preface). Prejudices: the idea that religion and morality can judge history. This prejudice was in principle in harmony with certain of the proponents of natural law. But also a prejudice: the idea that the abstraction of a political ideal, even dressed up in the principles of science, can stand in for history. In this Montesquieu broke absolutely with the theoreticians of natural law. Rousseau made no mistake about it: 'The science of politics is and probably always will be unknown. . . . In modern times the only man who could have created this vast and useless science was the illustrious Montesquieu. But he was not concerned with the principles of political law; he was content to deal with the positive laws of settled governments; and nothing could be more different than these two branches of study. Yet he who would judge wisely in matters of actual government is forced to combine the two; he must know what ought to be in order to judge what is.'[8]

The Montesquieu who refuses precisely to judge what is by what ought to be, who only wants to give the real necessity of history the form of its law, by drawing this law from the diversity of the facts and their variations, this man is indeed *alone* in facing his task.

8. *Émile*, translated by B. Foxley (London, 1957), v, pp. 421–2.

Chapter Two

A New Theory of Law

A refusal to subordinate the material of political facts to religious and moral principles, a refusal to subordinate it to the abstract concepts of the theory of natural law, which are nothing but disguised value judgements, that is what clears away the prejudices and opens the royal road of science. That is what introduces Montesquieu's great theoretical revolutions.

The most famous of these is contained in two lines defining *laws*: 'Laws . . . are the necessary relations arising from the nature of things' (SL, I, I). The theologian of the *Defence*, who is not so naïve as Montesquieu would have us think, cannot believe his eyes. 'The laws relations – what can he mean by this? The author has not however deviated from the ordinary definition of Laws without design.'[1] He was right. Montesquieu's intention, whatever he may have said, was certainly to change something in the received definition.

The long history of the concept of law is well-known. Its modern meaning (the sense of *scientific law*) only emerged in the works of the physicists and philosophers of the sixteenth and seventeenth centuries. And even then it still carried with it the traits of its past. Before taking the new sense of a constant relation between phenomenal variables, i.e. before relating to the practice of the modern experimental sciences, law belonged to the world of religion, morality and politics. It was, in its meaning, steeped in exigencies arising from human relations. Law thus presupposed human beings, or beings in the image of man, even if they surpassed it. The law was a *commandment*. It thus needed a will to

1. *A Defence of the S L*, Part I, I, Objection I.

order and wills to obey. A legislator and subjects. The law possessed thereby the structure of conscious human action: it had an *end*, it designated a target, at the same time as it required its attainment. For the subjects who lived *within the law* it offered the ambiguity of constraint and ideal. It is this meaning and its resonances that can be seen exclusively to dominate medieval thought, from Saint Augustine to Saint Thomas. Law having only one structure, divine law, natural laws and positive (human) laws could be discussed *in the same sense*. Every case exhibited the same form of commandment and end. Divine law dominated all laws. God had given his orders to nature as a whole and to man, and by doing so had fixed *their ends*. The other laws were no more than the echo of this primordial commandment, repeated more and more faintly throughout the universe, the communion of angels, human societies, nature. As we know, it is a fault of those who give orders, at least in certain institutions, to like them to be repeated.

It was a long time before the idea that nature might have laws which were not orders could rid itself of this heritage. It is visible in Descartes, who still tried to reduce to a divine decree the laws he had discovered only in bodies: conservation of motion, fall, collision. With Spinoza came the awareness of a first difference: 'But the application of the word "law" to natural things seems to be metaphorical,' for the 'ordinary meaning of law is simply a command.'[2] In the seventeenth century, this long effort succeeded in disengaging a special domain for this new meaning of law: the domain of *nature*, of *physics*. Sheltered by the divine decree which still protected from on high the old form of law, saving the appearances, a new form of law was developing which, little by little, through Descartes and Newton, took the form stated by Montesquieu: 'a fixed and invariable relation' between variable terms, such that 'each diversity is uniformity; each change is constancy' (SL, I, I). But it was hard to see how what is valid for falling or colliding bodies, and for the planets

2. *Theologico-Political Treatise*, IV, in Benedict de Spinoza, *The Political Works*, edited and translated by A. G. Wernham (Oxford, 1958), p. 69.

moving in their orbits, could be turned into a *universal model*. The old sense of law, which is an order and an end pronounced by a master, maintained its original position: the domain of divine law, the domain of moral (or natural) law, the domain of human laws. And one can even note something at first sight paradoxical but rational enough: that the theoreticians of natural law whom I have discussed made their concepts a contribution to the old definition of law. Doubtless they, too, had 'secularized' 'natural law', the God who pronounced it or, having made his decision, mounted guard over it, being as useless as Descartes's God: no more than a night-watchman against thieves. But they had retained from the old version its teleological structure, its character as an ideal masked by the immediate appearances of *nature*. For them natural law was as much a *norm* (devoir) as a necessity. All their demands found refuge and support in a definition of law which was still foreign to the new one.

But in these two lines, Montesquieu proposes quite simply to expel the old version of the word law from the domains which it still held. And to consecrate the reign of the modern definition – law as a relation – over the whole extent of beings, from God to stones. 'In this sense, all beings have their laws; the Deity his laws, the material world its laws, the intelligences superior to man their laws, the beasts their laws, man his laws' (SL, I, I). Everything is in this sentence. At last an end has been put to all forbidden reserves. The scandal can well be imagined. No doubt God is still there to give the initial push, if not to mislead. He created the world. But he is no more than one of the terms of the relations. He is the 'primitive reason', but the laws put him on the same footing as beings: 'Laws are the relations subsisting between it (primitive reason, i.e. God) and different beings, and the relations of these to one another' (SL, I, I). Add to this the fact that God himself, the instituter of these laws, in creating beings sees his own primordial decree subordinated to a necessity of the same nature, and even God falls inwardly victim to the universal contagion of the law! If he did make these laws that govern the world, the ultimate reason is that 'they are relative to his wisdom and power'. Once God has been dealt with, the rest follows. The best way to reduce one's opponent is to bring him over to one's own side. He watched over the old domains. They have now been opened up to Montesquieu, and first of all the entire world of the existence of men in their cities and in their history. He is at last to be able to impose on them *his own law*.

We must face up to the implications of this theoretical revolution. It presupposes that it is possible to apply a Newtonian category of law to matters of politics and history. It presupposes that it is possible to draw from human institutions themselves the wherewithal to think their diversity in a uniformity and their changes in a constancy: the law of their diversification and the law of their development. This law will no longer be an ideal order but instead a relation immanent to the phenomena.[3] It will not be given in the intuition of essences, but drawn from the facts themselves, without preconceived ideas, by investigation and comparison, by trial and error. At the moment of its discovery, it will be no more than a *hypothesis*, and will only become a principle once it has been verified by the utmost diversity of phenomena: 'I have followed my object without any fixed plan; I have known neither rules nor exceptions; I have found the truth only to lose it again. But, when I had once discovered my first principles, every thing I fought for appeared' (SL, Preface). 'I have laid down the first principles, and have found that the particular cases apply naturally to them; that the histories of all nations are only consequences of them' (ibid.). This is indeed the cycle of an empirical science in search of the law of its object, almost to the point of direct experimentation.

But this theoretical revolution also presupposes that the object of scientific observation (here the civil and political laws of human societies) is not confused with the results of the investiga-

---

3. A clear Newtonian resonance in Montesquieu's formulations: the author, he says of himself, 'is not treating of causes, nor does he compare causes: but he treats of effects, and compares effects' (*A Defence of the SL*, Part I, I, The Answer to Objection III). Cf. also the following note on polygamy: 'It is not an affair of calculation, when we reason on its nature; it may be an affair of calculation, when we combine its effects' (ibid., Part II, Of Polygamy).

tion itself: that there is no play on the word *law*. This dangerous confusion is inherent in the fact that Montesquieu, who with all objects of knowledge disengages their *laws* from the facts, is here seeking to know a particular object, the positive *laws* of human societies. But the laws found in Greece in the fifth century B.C. or in the Kingdom of the First Frankish Line, are obviously not laws in the first sense – scientific laws. They are juridical institutions, for which Montesquieu wants to state the (scientific) law of their distribution and evolution. He says this quite plainly when he distinguishes between *laws* and *their spirit*: 'I do not pretend to treat of laws, but of their spirit, and . . . this spirit consists in the various relations which the laws may have to different objects' (SL, I, 3). Thus Montesquieu does not confuse the laws of his object (the *spirit* of laws) with his object itself (*laws*). I believe that this simple distinction is indispensable if a certain misunderstanding is to be avoided. Still in Book I, having shown that all the beings of the universe and even God are subject to laws as relations, Montesquieu envisages *the differences in their modalities*. In this way, he distinguishes between the laws that govern inanimate matter, and which brook not the slightest deviation, and the laws that govern beasts and men. As one rises in the scale of being, laws lose their fixity and at any rate their observation its precision. 'The intelligent world is far from being so well governed as the physical' (SL, I, I). Thus man, who has over other beings the privilege of *knowledge*, is prone to error and the passions. Hence his disobedience: 'As an intelligent being, he incessantly transgresses the laws established by God, and changes those of his own institution' (SL, I, I). Worse still, he does not even observe those he has given himself! But it is precisely this errant being, in its history, that is the object of Montesquieu's investigations: a being whose conduct does not always obey the laws it is given, and in addition can have special laws it has made: positive laws, without for all that respecting them any more than the others.

These reflections may seem in Montesquieu's case those of a moralist deploring man's weakness. I believe rather that they are those of a theoretician who is here confronting a profound ambiguity. Indeed, *two different interpretations* can be given of this distinction between the modalities of laws, two interpretations which represent two tendencies in Montesquieu himself.

In the first, one could say: sticking firmly to the methodological principle that the laws of relation and variation that can be disengaged from human laws are distinct from those laws themselves, men's errors and deviations with respect to those laws raise no problems. The sociologist, unlike the physicist, is not dealing with an object (a body) which is obedient to a simple determinism and follows a line from which it does not deviate – but with a very special type of object: men who deviate even from the laws they give themselves. What then has to be said about men and their relation to their laws? That they change them, get round them or violate them. But none of this affects the idea that it is possible to disengage from their obedient or rebellious conduct a law that they follow *without knowing it*, and from their very errors, the truth of this law. To be discouraged in the search for the laws of men's conduct one must be so simple as to take the laws they give themselves for the necessity governing them! In truth, their error, the aberrations of their humour, their violation and changing of their laws, are quite simply part of their *conduct*. All that is required is to disengage the laws of the violation of laws, or of their changing. And this is indeed what Montesquieu does in almost every chapter of the *Spirit of Laws*. Open a book on history (the Roman succession, justice in the early period of feudalism, etc.): it is clear that its object consists precisely of human divagation and variation. This attitude already presupposes a very fruitful methodological principle, the refusal to take the motives of human action for its dynamic, the ends and arguments men consciously propose to themselves for the real, most often unconscious causes which make them act. Montesquieu thus appeals constantly to causes of which men are *ignorant*: climate, soil, manners and morals, the inner logic of a set of institutions, etc., precisely so as to explain human laws and the deviation which separates men's conduct both from 'primitive' laws (the natural laws of morality) and from *positive* laws. Everything goes to show that Montesquieu did not intend to state the 'spirit' of laws, i.e. the law of laws, without also stating the bad human side of the spirit of laws: the law of their violation, in one and the same principle.

This interpretation allows us to give a perhaps more apt sense to a theme which constantly recurs in Montesquieu, and which seems to concern the norms (*devoirs*) governing laws. Indeed, when discussing human laws, we very often find Montesquieu appealing from existing laws to better ones. A strange paradox for a man who refuses to judge what is by what ought to be (*doit être*) – and yet falls into the trap that he himself has denounced! Montesquieu says for example (and this clashes with all the laws deprived of that reason he describes in his book) that 'law in general is human reason, in as much as it governs all the peoples of the earth' (SL, I, 3). He also says that laws *ought to be* adapted to the people, that they *ought to be* relative to the nature and principle of the government, that they *ought to be* relative to the physical constitution of the country, etc. The list of these 'oughts' or norms is endless. And just when one thinks one has properly grasped the essence of his definition of the nature and principle of a government, one is astonished to read that this 'does not imply, that, in a particular republic, they actually are, but that they ought to be, virtuous . . . otherwise the government is imperfect' (SL, III, 11). Despotism itself, to be 'perfect', God knows by what sort of perfection, has itself some norms to respect! The general conclusion from these texts seems to be: the theoretician of the ideal, or the legislator, has taken the place of the scientist. The latter only wanted facts; the former proposes ends. But here again the misunderstanding depends in part on a word-play on the two *laws*: the laws really ordering the actions of men (the laws the scientist is investigating) and the laws ordained by men. When Montesquieu proposes norms for the laws, this is only for the laws that men provide themselves. These 'norms' are quite simply a demand for men to narrow the distance between the laws that govern men unbeknownst to them and the laws they make and know. It is indeed an appeal to the legislator, but an appeal for him, aware of the illusions of ordinary consciousness and critical of that blind consciousness, to model himself on the enlightened consciousness of the scientist, i.e. on science, and to make the conscious laws he gives men conform as far as possible to the unconscious laws that govern them. Hence it is not a question of an abstract ideal, of an infinite task which concerns men because they are impotent and errant beings. It is a question of a *correction of errant consciousness by well-founded science*, of the unconscious consciousness by the scientific consciousness. Hence it is a question of transferring the acquisitions of science into political practice itself, correcting the errors and unconsciousness of that practice.

Such is the first of the two possible interpretations, and it illuminates the immense majority of Montesquieu's examples. Thus understood, Montesquieu is indeed the conscious precursor of all modern political science, which will have none of any but a critical science, which only disengages the real laws of the conduct of men from the apparent laws they provide for themselves in order to criticize those apparent laws and modify them, thus returning to history the results obtained in the knowledge of history. This scientific distance with respect to history and this conscious return to history can, of course, if the object of the science is taken for the science itself, provide a pretext for the accusation of *political idealism* (cf. Poincaré: science is in the indicative; action in the imperative)! But once it is clear that the distance described as *ideal* between the existing state and the project of its reform is in this case simply the *distance of a science from its object* and from ordinary consciousness, every objection of this kind falls. In the apparent *ideal* that science proposes for its object, it is merely restoring to it what it had taken from it: its own distance, which is knowledge itself.

But I have to admit that there is *another possible interpretation* of the texts I have been discussing, and one that can be sustained in Montesquieu himself. Here indeed is the way he introduces human laws into the concert of general laws: 'Particular intelligent beings may have laws of their own making; but they have some likewise which they never made. Before there were intelligent beings, they were possible; they had therefore possible relations, and consequently possible laws. Before laws were made, there were relations of possible justice. To say that there is nothing just or unjust, but what is commanded or forbidden by positive laws, is the same as saying that, before the describing of a circle, all the radii were not equal. We must therefore acknowledge relations of justice antecedent to the positive law by which they are established' (SL, I, I). And these 'primitive' laws are related to God. These laws of an always pre-existent justice, independent of all the concrete conditions of history, amount to the old type of commandment-law, normative law. It matters little whether they are called divine and are exercised by the ministrations of natural religion; or moral and are exercised by the education of fathers and teachers or by the voice of nature which Montesquieu, before Rousseau, called 'the sweetest of all sounds' (SL, XXVI, 4); or political. It is no longer a question of the positive human laws engaged in concrete conditions of existence from which the scientist has to disengage precisely *their law*. It is a question of a norm established for man by nature or God, which amounts to the same thing. And this characteristic contains, of course, a confusion of orders: scientific law disappears behind command-ment-law. This temptation can be detected very distinctly at the end of the first chapter of Book I. The quotations I have used to support the first interpretation then tend in a completely new direction. It is just as if, now, human error, that integral part of men's conduct, was no longer an object of the science, but the profound argument justifying the existence of laws, i.e. of norms. It would be amusing to imagine that the reason why bodies do not have (positive) laws is because they do not have the wit to disobey their laws! For the reason men do have such laws is less because of their imperfection (who would not give all the stones in the world for a man?) than because of their capacity for insubordination. Man: 'He is left to his private direction, though a limited being, and subject, like all finite intelligences, to ignorance and error: even his imperfect knowledge he loseth; and, as a sensible creature, he is hurried away by a thousand impetuous passions. Such a being might every instant forget his Creator; God has therefore reminded him of his duty by the laws of religion. Such a being is liable every moment to forget himself; philosophy has provided against this by the laws of morality. Formed to live in society, he might forget his fellow-creatures; legislators have, therefore, by political and civil laws, confined him to his duty' (sL, 1 1). This time we have really fallen back, no question. These laws are orders. They are laws against forgetfulness, *laws of recall* which restore to man his memory, i.e. his duty or norms, range him with the end he has to pursue, whether he will or no, if he wants to fulfil his destiny as a man. These laws no longer concern the relation between man and his conditions of existence, but rather *human nature*. The normative margin in these laws no longer, as above, concerns the distance between the human unconsciousness and the consciousness of its laws, it concerns the *human condition*. Human nature, human condition, here we are right back in a world we thought we had broken with. In a world of values fixed in heaven in order to draw to them the gaze of men.

Here Montesquieu returns like a good boy to the most insipid of traditions. Eternal values do exist. Read the statement of this in Book 1: the laws must be obeyed; one's benefactor must be recognized; one's Creator must be obeyed; evil deeds will be punished. A remarkable list! A second one complements it: Book 1, Chapter 2, teaching that 'nature' gives us the idea of a Creator and inclines us towards him; that it intends that we should live in peace; that we should eat; that we should be inclined towards the other sex; and be desirous of living in society. The rest is added bit by bit, scattered as it is in more remote passages: that a father owes his offspring nourishment, but not necessarily inheritance; that a son supports his father if he is in trouble; that women must give way to men in the home; and above all that behaviour relating to modesty is all important in human purposes (whether it is a question of women in most of their actions, in marriage combinations, or the conjugation of the two sexes in abominable encounters); that despotism and torture conflict with human nature always, and slavery often. In short, a number of liberal demands, some more political ones, and many platitudes in support of well-established customs. Nothing remotely resembling the generous attitudes that other no less prudish, but more resolute or naïve theorists attributed or were to attribute to 'human nature': liberty, equality, fraternity. We really are in another world.

I believe that this side of Montesquieu is not a matter of indifference. It does not amount only to one isolated *concession* in a set of rigorous exigencies, the tribute paid to satisfy the world's prejudices, in order to have peace. *Montesquieu needed this recourse and refuge.* As he needed the ambiguity of his conception of law to combat his most ferocious opponents. Re-read his reply to the watchful theologian. These laws which precede themselves, these equal radii equal for all eternity, before anyone, God or man, had ever drawn a circle anywhere, these relations of equity predating all possible positive laws, provide him with an argument against the Hobbesian threat. 'The Author was attempting to overthrow Hobbes's system; a system the most terrible, in that by making all the virtues and vices depend on the establishment of laws men make for themselves . . . he, like Spinoza, overthrows both all religion and all morality.'[4] So much for religion and morality. But something quite different is at stake. No longer the laws controlling religion and morality, but the laws governing *politics*, decisive laws for Montesquieu himself. It is the foundation of these laws that is at stake for Hobbes in the contract. These eternal laws of Montesquieu's, laws pre-existing all human laws, are thus really the refuge in which he protects himself from his opponent. That there were laws before laws makes it clear that *there is no longer a contract*, nor any of the political perils to which the very idea of a contract commits men and governments. In the shelter of the eternal laws of a nature without egalitarian structure, one can fight the opponent from afar. He can be awaited on the

4. *A Defence of the S L*, Part I, I, The Answer to Objection I.

terrain of *nature*, a terrain, however, that one has chosen before him, and with the appropriate weapons. Everything is prepared for the defence of a different cause from nature's: that of a shaken world one would like to re-establish on its foundations.

It is certainly not the least of Montesquieu's paradoxes that he thus served old causes with ideas the strongest of which were completely new. But it is time to follow him into his most familiar thoughts, which are also his most secret ones.

Chapter Three

The Dialectic of History

Everything I have said so far concerns only Montesquieu's method, its presuppositions and meaning. This method applied to his object is indisputably novel. But a method, even a novel one, may be in vain *if it fails to produce anything new*. What then are Montesquieu's positive discoveries?

'I have first of all considered mankind; and the result of my thoughts has been, that, amidst such an infinite diversity of laws and manners, they were not solely conducted by the caprice of fancy. I have laid down the first principles, and have found that the particular cases apply naturally to them; that the histories of all nations are only consequences of them; and that every particular law is connected with another law, or depends on some other of a more general extent' (SL, Preface). Such is Montesquieu's discovery: not *particular ingenuities* but universal first principles making intelligible the whole of human history and *all its particulars*: 'When once I had discovered my first principles, everything I sought for appeared' (ibid.).

What then are the principles which make history intelligible in this way? Once posed, this question raises a number of difficulties which directly involve the *make-up* of the *Spirit of Laws*. Montesquieu's great work, which opens with the pages I have just been discussing, does not indeed have the expected arrangement. First of all, from Book I to Book XIII, it contains a theory of governments and of the different laws that depend either on their natures or on their principles: in other words, a *typology*, which appears very abstract, although it is crammed with historical examples, and seems to constitute a whole isolated from the rest, 'a complete master-piece within an incomplete master-piece' (J. J. Chevallier). After Book XIII we seem to enter another world. Everything should have been said about the governments, their types being known, but here we have the climate (Books XIV, XV, XVI, XVII), then the quality of the soil (Book XVIII), then manners and morals (Book XIX), and commerce (Books XX, XXI), and money (Book XXII), and population (Book XXIII) and finally religion (Books XXIV, XXV), which each in turn determine the laws whose secret has apparently already been provided. And to cap the confusion, four Books of history, one discussing the development of the Roman laws of succession (Book XXVII), three expounding the origins of feudal laws (Books XXVIII, XXX, XXXI), and between them one Book on the 'manner of composing laws' (Book XXIX). Principles which claim to provide order for history ought at least to put some of it in the treatise which expounds them.

Where indeed are they to be found? The *Spirit of Laws* seems to be made up of three parts added on to one another, like ideas which have come up and that one does not want to lose. Where is the clear unity we expected? Should we seek Montesquieu's 'principles' in the first thirteen Books, and thus owe him the idea of *a pure typology of the forms of government*, the description of their peculiar dynamic, the deduction of laws as a function of their nature and principle? Suppose we agree. But then all the material about climate and the various factors, then the history, seem interesting certainly, but additional. Are the true principles on the contrary in the *second part*, in the idea that the laws are determined by different factors, some material (climate, soil, population, economy), others moral (manners and morals, religion)? But then what is the concealed argument linking these determinant principles with the first ideal principles and the final historical studies? Any attempt to maintain the whole in an impossible unity, the ideality of the types, the determinism of the material or moral environment, and the history, falls into irresoluble contradictions. Montesquieu could be said to be torn between a mechanistic materialism and a moral idealism, between atemporal structures and a historical genesis, etc. Which is a way of saying that if he did make *certain* discoveries, they are only linked by the disorder of his book, which proves against him that he did not make *the particular* discovery he thought he had made.

I should like to try to combat this impression and reveal between the different 'truths' of the *Spirit of Laws* the *chain that links them to other truths* discussed in the Preface.

The first expression of Montesquieu's new principles is to be found in the few lines which distinguish between the *nature* and the *principle* of a government. Each government (republic, monarchy, despotism) has *its nature* and *its principle*. Its *nature* is 'that by which it is constituted', its *principle* the passion 'by which it is made to act' (SL, III, 1).

What is to be understood by the *nature* of a government? The *nature* of the government answers the question: *who holds power? how does the holder of power exercise that power?* Thus, the *nature* of republican government implies that the body of the nation (or a part of the nation) has sovereign authority. The *nature* of monarchical government, that one alone governs, but by fixed and established laws. The *nature* of despotism, that one alone governs, but with neither laws nor rules. The retention and mode of exercise of power – all this remains purely legal, and when all is said and done, *formal*.

The *principle* takes us into life. For a government is not a pure form. It is the concrete form of existence of a society of men. For the men subject to a particular type of government to be precisely and lastingly subject to it, the mere imposition of a political form (*nature*) is not enough, they must also have a disposition to that form, a certain way of acting and reacting which will underpin that form. As Montesquieu puts it, there has to be a specific *passion*. Each form of government necessarily desires its own passion. The republic wants virtue, monarchy honour, and despotism fear. The principle of a government is drawn from its form, for it is a 'natural' derivation of it. But this consequence is less its *effect* than its *precondition*. Take the example of the republic. The *principle* of the republic, virtue, answers the question: *on what condition can there be a government which gives power to the people and makes it exercise that power by the laws?* – On the condition that the citizens are *virtuous*, i.e. sacrifice themselves to the public good, and, in all circumstances, prefer the fatherland to their own passions. The same for monarchy and despotism. If the *principle* of the government is its *spring, that which makes it act*, that is because it is, as the life of the government, quite simply its condition of existence. The republic will only 'go', to coin a phrase, on virtue, just as some motors will only go on petrol. Without virtue the republic will fall, as will monarchy without honour, despotism without fear.

Montesquieu has been accused of formalism because of his way of defining a government by its *nature*, which does indeed consist of a few words of pure constitutional law. But it is forgotten that *the nature of a government is formal for Montesquieu himself, so long as it is separated from its principle*. One should say: in a government a nature without a principle is inconceivable and non-existent. Only the *nature-principle totality* is conceivable, because it is real. And this totality is no longer formal, for it no longer designates a purely juridical form, but a political form engaged in its own life, in its own conditions of existence and survival. Although defined in one word, virtue, honour, fear, these conditions are highly concrete. Like passion in general, the passions may seem abstract, but *as principles they express politically the whole real life of the citizens*. The virtue of the citizen is his entire life devoted to the public good: this passion, dominant in the State, is, in one man, all his passions dominated. With the principle it is the concrete life of men, public and even private, that enters into the government. The *principle* is thus the intersection of the *nature* of the government (its political form) with the real life of men. It is thus *the point and aspect in which the real life of men has to be resumed in order to be inserted into the form of a government*. The principle is the concrete of that abstract, the nature. It is their unity, it is their totality, that is real. Where is the formalism?

This point will be conceded. But it is decisive if we are to grasp the full extent of Montesquieu's *discovery*. *In this idea of the*

*totality of the nature and the principle of a government, Montesquieu
is in fact proposing a new theoretical category*, one which gives him
the key to an infinity of riddles. Before him political theorists had
certainly tried to explain the multiplicity and diversity of the laws
of a given government. But they had done little more than outline
a logic of the *nature* of governments, even when they were not, as
in most cases, satisfied by a mere description of elements *without
any inner unity*. The immense majority of laws, such as those that
determine education, division of lands, degree of property,
techniques of justice, punishments and rewards, luxury, the
condition of women, the conduct of war, etc. (SL, IV–VII), were
excluded from this logic, because their *necessity* was not understood. Montesquieu here majestically closes this old debate, by
*discovering and verifying in the facts the hypothesis that the State is
a real totality and that all the particulars of its legislation, of its
institutions and its customs are merely the effect and expression of its
inner unity*. He submits these laws, which seem fortuitous and
irrational, to a profound logic, and relates them to a single centre.
I do not claim that Montesquieu was the first to think that the
State should of itself constitute a *totality*. This idea is already
lurking in Plato's reflection and we find it again at work in the
thought of the theoreticians of natural law, at any rate in Hobbes.
But before Montesquieu this idea only entered into the constitution of an *ideal* State, without lowering itself to the point of
making *concrete* history intelligible. With Montesquieu, the
totality, which was an *idea*, becomes a scientific *hypothesis*,
intended to *explain the facts*. It becomes the fundamental category
which makes it possible to think, no longer the reality of an ideal
state, but the concrete and hitherto unintelligible diversity of the
institutions of human history. History is no longer that infinite
space in which are haphazardly scattered the innumerable works
of caprice and accident, to the discouragement of the understanding, whose only possible conclusion is the insignificance of
man and the greatness of God. This space has a structure. *It
possesses concrete centres to which are related a whole local horizon of
facts and institutions: the States. And at the core of these totalities,*

which are like living individuals, there is an inner reason, an inner unity, a fundamental primordial centre: the unity of nature and principle. Hegel, who gave the category of the totality enormous scope well knew his own teacher when he expressed his gratitude for this discovery to Montesquieu's genius.

Here, however, formalism is still lying in wait for us. For it may well be that this category of the totality constituted the unity of the first Books of the *Spirit of Laws*. But it may be said that it is restricted to them, and that it is marked by the error of these first Books: that it concerns *pure models*, a truly republican republic, a truly monarchical monarchy and a truly despotic despotism only. In 'Reflections on the Preceding Chapters' (SL, III, 11), Montesquieu says: 'Such are the principles of the three sorts of government: which does not imply, that, in a particular republic, they actually are, but that they ought to be, virtuous: nor does it prove, that, in a particular monarchy, they are actuated by honour; or, in a particular despotic government, by fear; but that they ought to be directed by these principles, otherwise the government is imperfect.' Is this not to prove that *an idea which is only valid for pure models and perfect political forms* has been taken for a category applicable to all existing governments? Is it not to relapse into a theory of essences and into the ideal trap which was precisely what was to be avoided? Whereas one must, *as a historian*, necessarily explain *a certain* very imperfect republic or monarchy, not a *pure* republic or monarchy? If the totality is only valid for the purity, what use is the totality in history, which is impurity itself? Or, and this is the same aporia, how can one ever think history in a category attached in essence to pure atemporal models? We have come back to the difficulty of the disparity of the *Spirit of Laws:* how to unite the beginning and the end, the pure typology and the history?

I believe we should be careful not to judge Montesquieu by one sentence, but, as he forewarns us, take his work as a whole, without separating what he says in it from what he does. It is indeed very remarkable that this theoretician of pure models never (or hardly ever) in his work gives any but *impure* examples.

Even in the history of Rome, which is for him truly the most perfect experimental subject, a kind of 'pure substance' of historical experimentation, the ideal purity only had one moment, at the beginning, for all the rest of the time Rome lived in political impurity. It would surely be incredible if Montesquieu were unaware of such a contradiction. It must be that he does not think he is contradicting his principles, but that he is giving them a more profound meaning than they are attributed. I believe in fact that the category of the *totality* (and the *nature-principle* unity which is its core) is indeed a universal category, one which does not concern just the perfect adequacies: republic-virtue, monarchy-honour, despotism-fear. Manifestly, Montesquieu considers that *in any State, whether it is pure or impure, the law of this totality and its unity is supreme*. If the State is pure, the unity will be an *adequate* one. But if it is impure, it will be a *contradictory* one. All the impure majority of Montesquieu's historical examples are so many examples of this contradictory unity. Thus Rome, once the first period is over, and the first great conquests have occurred, lives in the State of a republic which will lose, loses and then has lost its principle: virtue. To say that therefore the nature-principle unity always survives but has become a contradiction is quite simply to state that *it is the relationship existing between the political form of a government and the passion then providing it with a content which governs the fate of that State*, its life, its survival, its future, and hence its historical essence. If this relationship is a *non-contradictory* one, i.e. if the republican form finds virtue in the men it governs, the republic will survive. But if this republican form is now only imposed on men who have abdicated all virtue and relapsed into private interests and passions, etc., then the relation will be a contradictory one. But it is precisely *this contradiction in the relation, i.e. the existing contradictory relation*, that decides the fate of the republic: it will perish. All this can be inferred from Montesquieu's historical studies, and in particular from *Considerations on the Causes of the Grandeur and Declension of the Roman Empire*, but it is also clearly stated in Book VIII of the *Spirit of Laws*, which deals with the corruption of governments. To say, as Montesquieu does, that a government which loses its principle is a lost government means quite clearly that the nature-principle unity is also supreme in the *impure* cases. If it were not, it would be impossible to understand how this broken unity could break its government.

Hence it is a strange mistake to doubt that Montesquieu has a sense of history, or to suspect that his typology diverted him from a theory of history, that he wrote books on history through a distraction which led him away from his principles. This mistake is no doubt rooted primarily in the fact that Montesquieu did not share the already widespread and soon to be dominant ideology, the belief that history has an end, is in pursuit of the realm of reason, liberty and 'enlightenment'. *Montesquieu was probably the first person before Marx who undertook to think history without attributing to it an end*, i.e. without projecting the consciousness of men and their hopes onto the time of history. This criticism is thus entirely to his credit. *He was the first to propose a positive principle of universal explanation for history;* a principle which is not just *static:* the totality explaining the diversity of the laws and institutions of a given government; but also *dynamic:* the law of the unity of nature and principle, a law making it possible to think the development of institutions and their transformations in real history, too. In the depth of the countless laws which come and go, he thus discovered a *constant connection* uniting the nature of a government to its principle; and at the core of this constant connection, he stated the inner variation of the relation, which, by the transitions of the unity from adequacy to inadequacy, from identity to contradiction, makes intelligible the changes and revolutions in the concrete totalities of history.

But Montesquieu was also the first to give an answer to a question which has become classic, the question of the *motor of history*. Let us look again at the law of historical development. It is completely governed by the *relation* existing between the nature and the principle in their very unity. If these two terms are in harmony (Republican Rome and virtuous Romans), the totality of the State is peaceful, men live in a history without crises. If the two terms are in contradiction (Republican Rome and Romans who have abandoned virtue), crisis breaks out. The principle is then no longer what is *wanted* by the nature of the government. Whence a chain reaction: the form of the government tries blindly to reduce the contradiction, it changes, and its change drags the principle along with it, until, with the help of circumstances, a new harmony emerges (imperial-despotic Rome and Romans living in fear), or a catastrophe which is the end of this breathless chase (barbarian conquest). The dialectic of this process is quite clear: its extreme moments are, either peace between the two terms of the opposition, or their conflict; in their conflict, the interaction of the terms is clear, as is how each modification of one inevitably induces a modification of the other. Thus it is clear that *nature and principle are absolutely interdependent in the mobile but pregnant totality of the State.* But it is not clear where the first change comes from, nor the last one, either in the order of *time*, or in that of *causes*. It is not clear *which* of these two terms linked together in the fate of the totality *is the preponderant one.*

In his work on the *Philosophy of the Enlightenment*, Ernst Cassirer praises Montesquieu for having thus founded a quite modern 'comprehensive' theory of history, i.e. for having thought history within the category of the *totality*, and the elements of this totality in a specific unity, *while precisely renouncing the idea that one element might be more important than the others*, i.e. that there might be a *motor of history*. History is simply a moving totality, whose unity can be *understood* and the *meaning* of whose inner movements can be grasped, but which can never be *explained*, i.e. its interactional movements can never be related to a determinant element. And in fact this view seems to accord with the letter of many passages from Montesquieu, who constantly turns from the form of the government to its principle, and from its principle to its form. It is the republican laws that produce the very virtue that enables them to be republican; the monarchical institutions that engender the honour that underpins them. As honour is for nobility, the principle is *both father and child of the form of government.* That is why every particular form produces in its principle its own conditions of existence, and always forestalls itself, although at the same time it is the principle which is expressed in that form. We would seem here to be in a real *circular expressive totality* in which each part is like the whole: *pars totalis.* And the movement of this sphere which we think is moved by a cause is no more than its displacement onto itself. With a rolling ball, each point on its sphere can move from top to bottom and return from there to the top, go back down again, and so on to infinity. But all its points do the same. There is neither top nor bottom in a sphere, entirely contained as it is in each of its points.

However, I believe that this slightly over-modern intuition does not express Montesquieu's most profound thought. For he intends there to be in the last instance *a determinant term : the principle.*

'The force of the principles draws everything to it.' Such is the grand lesson of Book VIII, which opens with the sentence, 'The Corruption of each government generally begins with that of the principles.' Corruption (and thus the impure state I have been discussing) constitutes a sort of experimental situation which makes it possible to penetrate the indivisible nature-principle unity and decide *which is the decisive element of the opposition.* The result is that it is definitely the principle that governs the nature and gives it its meaning. 'When once the principles of government are corrupted, the very best laws become bad, and turn against the state: but, when the principles are sound, even bad laws have the same effect as good' (SL, VIII, 11). 'A State may alter two different ways; either by the amendment, or by the corruption, of the constitution. If it has preserved its principles, and the constitution changes, this is owing to its amendment; if, upon changing the constitution, its principles are lost, this means that it has been corrupted' (SL, XI, 13). This clearly shows the transition from the case of the experimental situation of corruption to the general case of any modification (to the good as well as to the bad) in the nature of the State. Thus it really is the principle which is, in the last resort, the cause of the development of forms and their meanings. To the point that the classic image of form and content (form being what informs, effectivity itself) has to be inverted. It is the principle that is, in this sense, the true form of that apparent form, the nature of the government. 'There are very few laws which are not good, while the State retains its principles. Here I may apply what Epicurus said of riches: "It is not the liquor, but the vessel, that is corrupted" ' (SL, VIII, 11).

Of course, this does not exclude *the effectivity of the nature on the principle*, but within certain limits. Otherwise it would be difficult to understand how Montesquieu could have imagined laws intended to preserve or reinforce the principle. The urgency of these laws is simply a confession of their *subordinate* character: they are only active in a domain which may escape them not only for a thousand accidental and external reasons, but also and above all for the fundamental reason that it reigns over them and decides even what they mean. There are thus limit situations in which laws that are intended to *provide manners and morals* are powerless against manners and morals themselves, and rebound against the end they were supposed to serve – the manners and morals rejecting laws opposed to their own goals. However hazardous a comparison it may be, and one that I put forward with all possible precautions, the type of this *determination in the last instance by the principle*, determination which nevertheless farms out a whole zone of subordinate effectivity to the *nature* of the government, can be compared with the type of determination which Marx attributes *in the last instance to the economy*, a determination which nevertheless farms out a zone of subordinate effectivity to *politics*. In both cases it is a matter of a unity which may be harmonious or contradictory; in both cases this determination does nonetheless cede to the determined element a whole region of effectivity, but subordinate effectivity.

Hence this interpretation reveals a real unity between the first and last parts of the *Spirit of Laws*, between the typology and the history. But there remains one difficulty: the so varied second part, which introduces climate, soil, commerce, religion – surely it represents new principles, and heteroclite ones, which clash with the unity I have just demonstrated?

Let us first run through the new determinant factors suggested to us. Before climate (Book XIV), there is another important element, referred to on several occasions, and particularly in Book VIII: *the dimensions of the State*. The nature of a government depends on the geographical extent of its empire. A minute State will be republican, a moderate State monarchic and an immense State despotic. Here is a determination that seems to overthrow the laws of history, since geography decides its forms *directly*. Climate reinforces this argument, since this time it is the temperature of the air that distributes the empires, despotisms beneath violent skies, moderate governments beneath tender ones, and decides in advance which men will be free and which slaves. We learn that 'The empire of the climate is the first, the most powerful of all empires' (SL, XIX, 14), but at the same time that this empire can be conquered by well-conceived laws leaning on its excesses to protect men from its effects. A new cause then appears: *the nature of the soil* occupied by a nation. According to whether it is fertile or arid, the government there will be a government of one man or of many; according to whether it is mountainous or a plain, a continent or an island, liberty or slavery will be found to triumph there. But here again the causality invoked can be counteracted: 'Countries are not cultivated in proportion to their fertility, but to their liberty' (SL, XVIII, 3). But here are the *manners and morals* (*moeurs*) or general spirit of a nation, which add their effectivities to the others; then commerce and money, and finally religion. It is hard to avoid an impression of disorder, as if Montesquieu wanted to exhaust a series of principles he has discovered separately and then heaped together for want of any better order. 'Mankind are influenced by various causes; by the climate, by the religion, by the laws, by the maxims of government, by precedents, morals, and customs' (SL, XIX, 4). The unity of a profound law has turned into a plurality of causes. The totality is lost in a list.

I do not want to make it look as if I hoped to save Montesquieu from himself by forcing this disorder to appear as an order. But I should like to suggest briefly that in this disorder we can often glimpse something approaching an order which is not foreign to what has so far been established.

What is indeed remarkable in the majority of these factors, which either determine the very nature of the government (e.g. geographical extent, climate, soil) or a certain number of its laws, is the fact that they only act on their object *indirectly*. Take the example of the climate. The torrid climate does not produce the despot just like that, nor does the temperate the monarch. The climate only acts on the *temperament* of men, by way of a nice physiology which dilates or contracts the extremities and thereby affects the global sensitivity of the individual, imprinting on him peculiar needs and leanings, down to his style of conduct. It is *the men thus constituted and conditioned* who are apt for particular laws and governments. 'It is the variety of wants, in different climates, that first occasioned a difference in the manner of living, and thus gave rise to a variety of laws' (SL, XIV, 10). The *laws* produced by the climate are thus the *last effect* in a whole chain, whose *penultimate link*, the *product* of the climate and the cause of the laws, is the 'customary life' (*manière de vivre*) which is the outside of the 'manners and morals' (*moeurs*) (SL, XIX, 16). Look at the *soil*: if fertile lands are good for the government of one man alone, that is because the peasant there is too busy and too well-paid by his efforts to raise his nose from the ground and his pence. *Commerce*: it does not act directly on the laws but via the intermediary of the manners: 'Wherever there is commerce, there we meet with agreeable manners' (SL, XX, 1) – hence the peaceful spirit of commerce, its suitability to certain governments, its repugnance for others. As for *religion* itself, it seems to be part of another world than these completely material factors, but it acts nonetheless in the same way: by giving a nation ways of living the law and practising morality; it only concerns government through the behaviour of citizens and subjects. It is its mastery of fear that makes the Mahometan religion so apt for despotism: it provides it with slaves, ripe for slavery. It is its mastery of morality that makes the Christian religion accord so well with moderate government: 'We owe to Christianity, in government, a certain political law; and in war, a certain law of nations' (SL, XXIV, 3). Thus just when they are acting on the government and determining certain of its essential laws, all these causes, apparently so radically disparate, converge *on a common point :* the customs, morals and manners of being, feeling and acting that they confer on the men who live within their empire.

From their conjunction arises what Montesquieu calls *the spirit of a nation*. He does write: 'Mankind are influenced by various causes; by the climate, by the religion, etc.,' but only so as to conclude: 'from whence is formed a general spirit of the nation' (SL, XIX, 4).

Hence it is the *result :* the manners and morals, the general spirit of a nation, which determines either the form of the government or a certain number of its laws. The question then arises, *is this not an already familiar determination?* Indeed, remember what I have said of the *principle* of a government and of the depths of the concrete life of men it expresses. Considered not from the viewpoint of the *form* of the government, i.e. of its political exigencies, but from the viewpoint of its *content*, i.e. of its origins, *the principle is really the political expression of the concrete behaviour of men*, i.e. of their manners and morals, and spirit. Of course, Montesquieu does not say in so many words that the manners and morals or spirit of a nation constitute the very essence of the *principle* of its government. But he does set out from principles as the pure forms of the government: their truth appears in their corruption. When the *principle* is lost, it is clear that *manners and morals effectively take the place of principle :* that they are its loss or salvation. Take the republic, abandoned by virtue: there is no longer any respect for magistrates there, nor for old age, nor even for . . . husbands. 'No longer will there be any such things as manners, order, or virtue' (SL, VIII, 2). It would be hard to say more clearly that the *principle* (virtue) is simply the expression of the *manners*. Look at Rome: in its trials and reverses, with events shaking all the forms, it held fast: 'Rome was a ship held by two anchors, religion and manners, in the midst of a furious tempest' (SL, VIII, 13). Finally, look at modern States: 'Most of the European nations are still governed by manners and morals' (SL, VIII, 8), which is what saves them from despotism, partly already master of their laws. How can it be doubted that the manners and morals, vaster and more extensive than the principle, are nonetheless its real foundation and seat, when the same dialectic can be seen outlined between the manners and morals and the laws as between the principles and the nature of a government? 'Laws are established, manners are inspired; these proceed from a general spirit, those from a particular institution: now, it is as dangerous, nay, more so, to subvert the general spirit as to change a particular institution' (SL, XIX, 12), It is hard to see why it would be *more* dangerous to change the manners and morals than the laws if the manners and morals did not have the same advantage over the laws as the principle has over the nature: *that of determining them in the last resort.*[1] Hence the idea that recurs so frequently of a sort of primitive virtue of manners and morals. If 'a people always knows, loves and defends its manners more than its laws' (SL, X, 11), that is because these manners are more profound and primordial. Thus, among the earliest Romans, 'their manners were sufficient to secure the fidelity of their slaves; so that there was no necessity for laws' (SL, XV, 16). Later, 'as they then wanted manners and morals, they had need of laws'. And among primitive peoples themselves, if manners precede laws and stand in for them (SL, XVIII, 13), that is because in some sense they derive their 'origin from nature'. The form and style of conduct which are *expressed politically in the principle* can be reduced to this ultimate basis. This ultimate basis whose essential components Montesquieu lists as the climate, the soil, the religion, etc.

1. 'In all societies, which are simply a union of minds, a common character is formed. This universal soul adopts a way of thinking which is the effect of a chain of infinite causes which multiply and combine century by century. Once the tone has been given and received, it alone governs, and everything that sovereigns, magistrates, and peoples may do or imagine, whether it seems to conflict with the tone or to follow it, always relates to it, and it dominates even the total destruction [of the society]' (*Mes Pensées*).

It seems to me that this substantial analogy between the manners and morals and the principle also explains the strange circular causality of these *factors*, which seem at first sight completely mechanical. It is true that the climate and the soil, etc., determine certain laws. But they can be counteracted by them, and all the art of the enlightened legislator consists of playing on this necessity in order to beat it. If this recourse is possible it is because this determination *is not direct but indirect*, and that it is completely gathered together and concentrated in the manners and spirit of a nation, entering via the *principle*, which is the political abstraction and expression of the manners and morals, into the totality of the State. But since within this totality there is a certain possible action of the nature on the principle, and hence of the laws on the manners and morals and consequently on their components and causes, *it is not surprising that climate may give way to the laws*.

I know that counter-quotations will be used against me and that I shall be accused of giving Montesquieu the benefit of the doubt. However, it seems to me that all the reservations one might express turn on no more than a single point: the ambiguity of the concepts of *principle* and *manners and morals*. But I believe that this ambiguity is *real* in Montesquieu himself. I should say that it expresses simultaneously his wish to introduce the utmost clarity and necessity into history, but also in some sense his inability – not to speak of his *choice*. For if the region of the *nature* of a government is always perfectly sharply defined, if the dialectic of the nature-principle unity and contradiction, and the thesis of the primacy of principle, both emerge clearly from his examples, the concept of principle and the concept of manners and morals remain vague.

I said that the principle expresses the condition of existence of a government, and has the real life of men as its concrete background. The parallel causalities of the second part of the *Spirit of Laws* reveal to us the components of this real life, i.e. the real material and moral conditions of the existence of a government – and summarize them in the manners and morals which come to

the surface in the *principle*. But it is hard to see the transition
from the manners and morals to the principle, from the real
conditions to the political exigencies of the form of a government,
which come together in the *principle*. The very terms I used, such
as *the manners being expressed in the principles*, betray this difficulty
– for this *expression* is in some sense torn between its origin (the
manners and morals) and the exigencies of its end (the form of the
government). All Montesquieu's ambiguity is linked to this
tension. He did feel that the necessity of history could only be
thought in the unity of its forms and their conditions of existence,
and in the dialectic of that unity. But he grouped all these
conditions, *on the one hand in the manners and morals*, which are
indeed produced by real conditions, but whose concept remains
vague (the synthesis of all these conditions in the manners and
morals is no more than cumulative); and *on the other hand in the
principle*, which, divided between its real origins and the exigencies
of the political form it has to animate, *leans too often towards these
exigencies alone*.

It will be said that this contradiction and this ambiguity are
inevitable in a man who thinks in the concepts of his period and
cannot transcend the limits of the then established knowledges,
simply interrelating what he knows, and unable to seek in the
conditions he is describing a deeper unity, which would presuppose a complete *political economy*.[2] That is true. And it is
already remarkable that Montesquieu should have defined and
designated in advance in a brilliant conception of history an as
yet obscure zone barely illuminated by a vague concept: the zone
of *manners and morals* (*moeurs*), and behind it the zone of *the
concrete behaviour of men in their relations with nature and with
their past*.

But within him another man than the scientist took advantage
of this ambiguity. The man of a political party which needed

2. See Voltaire already: 'Montesquieu had no knowledge of the political principles
relating to wealth, manufactures, finances and commerce. These principles had not
yet been discovered. . . . It would have been as impossible for him to make [*The
Spirit of Laws*] Smith's treatise on wealth as Newton's mathematical principles.'

precisely the pre-eminence of the forms over their principles, and wanted there to be *three kinds of government*, in order that, protected by the necessities of climate, manners and morals, and religion, it could make its *choice* between them.

Chapter Four

'There are Three Governments . . .'

There are thus three species of government. The republic, monarchy and despotism. These totalities should be closely examined.

I. THE REPUBLIC

I hope to be very brief on the republic. Faguet may have said that Montesquieu is a republican. Montesquieu does not believe in the republic, and for a simple reason: *the age of republics is past.* Republics only last in small States. Our era is that of medium and large empires. Republics can only be sustained by virtue and frugality, general mediocrity in its original sense, i.e. that everybody is content with nothing. Our age is one of luxury and commerce. Virtue has become such a burden that its effects would be disastrous if they could not be attenuated by milder laws. For all these reasons, the republic retreats into the distant past: Greece, Rome. No doubt that is why it is so beautiful. Montesquieu, who is quite prepared to call Richelieu crazy for his claim to want an angel for king, so rare is virtue, accepts that in Greece and Rome there were, at certain periods, enough angels to make up whole cities.

This political angelicism makes democracy (for here I shall ignore aristocracy, which is an unstable mixture of democracy and monarchy) an exceptional regime, a kind of synthesis of all the exigencies of politics. First, it is truly a *political* regime, by which I mean a regime which attains the *true* sphere of politics: that of stability and universality. In democracy, the men who are 'everything' are nonetheless not at the mercy of their own caprice. The citizens are not so many despots. Their omnipotence subordinates them to a political order and a political structure which they recognize and which transcend them as individual men: the order of the laws, whether *fundamental*, i.e. constitutive of the regime, or occasional, i.e. decreed in response to events. But this order itself, which makes them *citizens*, is not an order received from without, as for example is the feudal order, the 'natural' inequality of the estates in a monarchy. In democracy, the citizens possess the unique privilege of themselves consciously and voluntarily producing in legislation the very order which governs them. Children of the laws, they are also their fathers. They are subjects only as sovereigns. They are masters subject to their own power. It is clear that this synthesis of subject and sovereign in the citizen, which haunted Rousseau, demands of man that he be more than man, and that without being quite an angel, he be a citizen, which is the true angel of public life.

This category of the citizen realizes the *synthesis of the State* in man himself: the citizen is the State in the private man. That is why *education* has such an important place in the economy of this regime (SL, IV, 5), for Montesquieu as well as for Rousseau. Montesquieu shows that democracy cannot tolerate the division of education characteristic of monarchic regimes. In fact modern man is torn between two educations: that of his fathers and teachers on the one hand, and that of the world on the other. The one preaches him morality and religion. The other never to forget himself. And what Hegel was to call *the law of the world*, which governs *real* human relations, triumphs over the law of the heart, whose refuge is the hearth and the Church (SL, IV, 4 & 5). None of this in a democratic regime: family, school and life speak the same language. The whole of life is simply an endless education. For, in its very essence, democracy presupposes, behind this endless discipline and edification which is in some sense its temporal form, a true *conversion* of the private man into the public man. If in democracy all private vices are public crimes, which is the justification for the censors, if civil law is identical with political law, that is because all of a man's private life consists of being a public man – the laws being the perpetual 'reminder' of this exigency. This circle of democracy, which is simply the eternal education of democracy, this remarkable circle of a regime which thus accepts its existence as a perpetual task, realizes the specific duty of the citizens, who, in order to be *all* as they are in the State, must, in their very persons, become 'all' of the State.

A moral conversion? That is what Montesquieu proposes when he depicts virtue, although it is entirely political, as the preference of the public good over private good (SL, III, 5; SL, IV, 5), as self-forgetfulness, as the triumph of reason over passion. But this moral conversion is not that of an isolated conscience, it is that of a State totally steeped in this duty, translated into *laws*. With its laws, the republic, which wants citizens, takes care to *force* them into virtue. At what cost can this virtue be thus forced? At the cost of an archaic economy maintained in its past, at the cost of manners and morals carefully guarded by the laws, the aged and the censors; lastly, and above all, at the cost of judicious political measures, which only aim to edify the people in order to maintain it within the power of its *notables*.

Indeed what is striking in the entirely retrospective apologia for the people's government constituted by *democracy* (aristocracy is much less exemplary, because, dare I say it, it is founded from the outset on the division of the people), is the care taken *to distinguish two peoples within the people*. When Montesquieu's republic is compared with Rousseau's, and the virtue of the one with the virtue of the other, it must not be forgotten that the former is in the past and the latter in the future; the latter a people's republic, the former a *republic of notables*. Hence the importance of the problem of *popular representation*. Rousseau has no intention that the people should legislate through its *representatives*: 'Sovereignty, for the same reason as makes it inalienable, cannot be represented; it lies essentially in the general will, and will does not admit of representation' (*The Social Contract*, Book III, Ch. 15).[1] A democracy which adopts repre-

1. Rousseau, *The Social Contract and Discourses*, op. cit., p. 78.

sentatives is on its death-bed. Montesquieu, on the contrary, holds that a democracy without representatives is an imminent popular despotism. This is because he has a very special idea of the people, confirmed by those ancient democracies in which the freedom of the 'free men' was to the forefront, leaving the multitude of artisans and slaves in the shade. Montesquieu does not want this 'common people' (*bas-peuple*) to have power.[2] This is indeed his most deep-lying concern, and it illuminates all the precautions of Book II (Chapter 2). Abandoned to itself, the people (the common people) is nothing but passion. It is incapable of foresight, thought and judgement. How could passion judge, since it is the very absence of reason? Let the people therefore be deprived of all direct power, but let them choose *representatives*. They are extremely well-qualified for choosing, for they see men in action at close quarters, and discern the good and the mediocre instantly. They know how to choose the good general, the good rich man and the good judge; they see the first in his wars, the second in his banquets and the third in his judgements. They have a 'natural capacity, in respect to the discernment of merit', and as proof that merit stares them in the face, 'though the people of Rome assumed to themselves the right of raising plebeians to public offices, yet they would never exert this power; and though, at Athens, the magistrates were allowed, by the law of Aristides, to be elected from all the different classes of inhabitants, there never was a case, says Xenophon, that the common people petitioned for employments which could endanger either their security or their glory' (SL, II, 2)! What a wonderful natural gift of the people, forcing them to admit their own inability even to be their own masters, and to take for lords precisely those who have the advantages of rank and fortune over them. Ancient democracy itself thus already witnesses in favour of all the notables of history.

Thus in democracy there is available what is required to rein-

---

2. 'There is nothing in the world more insolent than republics. . . . The common people is the most insolent tyrant there can be', *Voyages* (Pléiade edition, 2 vols, ed. Roger Caillois, Paris, 1949–51, vol. I, p. 863).

force this judicious inclination and, if all else fails, what is required to admonish it and establish it in its vocation. In particular, there are laws which divide the people into classes, with enough discrimination to deprive the commoners of their votes. 'It is in the manner of making this division that great legislators have signalized themselves.' Servius Tullius, for example, had the wit to 'lodge the right of suffrage in the hands of the principal citizens', so that 'it was property rather than numbers that decided the elections'. Or the Roman legislators who realized that the public vote 'should be considered as a fundamental law of democracy', for, 'the lower classes ought to be directed by those of higher rank, and restrained within bounds by the gravity of eminent personages' (SL, 11, 2). Voting *secretly* is a privilege of the aristocratic seigneury, for the reason that they are themselves their own great men! No doubt but that the surest means of maintaining such a *natural* disposition is to produce it.

Carefully confined to the past by the enlargement of modern States and the turn of events which has made virtue inhuman, democracy therefore only relates to the present by the lessons of experience that descend from it: 'Even in a popular government, the power ought not to fall into the hands of the common people' (SL, XV, 18).

2. MONARCHY

With monarchy and despotism, which is in some sense its inverse and pole of attraction, we are *in the present*. Montesquieu thinks that modern times belong to feudal monarchy, and the feudal monarchy belongs to modern times. Antiquity knew no real monarchies (in Rome, as we know, the republic was what was hidden in its trappings) for two reasons, which their conjunction will illuminate: because it was ignorant of the true distribution of powers and knew nothing of government by the nobility.

What is monarchy? By its *nature* it is the government of a single person who directs the State 'by fixed and established laws'. By its *principle*, it is the reign of *honour*.

A single person who governs: the king. But what are these laws which have the privilege of being *fixed and established*? What is the meaning of this fixity and establishment? Here Montesquieu has in mind what jurists had for three centuries called the *fundamental laws of the kingdom*. The expression *fundamental law* often appears in the *Spirit of Laws*. Every government has its fundamental laws. Thus the republic has, among others, the electoral law. Thus despotism has the nomination of a vizir by the despot. We even learn in passing that the *colonial pact* is the fundamental law of Europe *vis-à-vis* its overseas colonial possessions (SL, XXI, 21). Thus Montesquieu uses the expression in a very broad way, assigning to it the designation of those laws in a government that define and found its 'nature' (in modern terms: its constitution), as distinct from the laws by which the government governs. But it is obvious that in the case of a monarchy this expression contains the echoes of past disputes. The object of these disputes was the definition of the powers of the *absolute monarch*. The notion of the fundamental laws of the kingdom intervened to limit the pretensions of the king. It demonstrated to him that he was king, by the grace of God no doubt, but also as an effect of laws older than him which he accepted tacitly by mounting the throne: the virtue of these laws seating him there even unbeknownst to him. The jurists usually cited the law of blood succession, but also a whole series of dispositions whose object was the recognition of the existing orders: nobility, clergy, parliament, etc. The fundamental laws which set the king on his throne demanded in return that the king respect them. It is to this meaning that Montesquieu is reverting under cover of a more general sense, when he talks of monarchy.

Read carefully Book 11 Chapter 4. You will find that the first sentence identifies the *nature* of monarchical government, government 'by fundamental laws', and the 'intermediate, subordinate, and dependent powers'. The intermediary powers are two in number: the nobility and the clergy, the nobility being the 'most natural' of the two. Thus 'intermediary bodies' are to be laws! Elsewhere Montesquieu cites as a fundamental law of monarchy the law of succession to the throne, which prevents intrigue and the dissipation of power, not only on the death, but also during the life of a prince. This law really is a law. He also invokes the necessity of a 'depository of the laws' independent of the royal authority, and this really is a matter of a 'law' establishing a *political* institution. But the nobility and the clergy! We were thinking of *political* institutions, and here we have the intervention of *social* orders. In fact the word *law* here only designates the privileged bodies in order to signify that the king is only the king through the existence of the nobility and the clergy, and that in return he must recognize them and defend their privileges.

This is all admitted straightaway: 'The most natural intermediate and subordinate power is that of the nobility. This, in some measure, seems to be essential to a monarchy, whose fundamental maxim is "No monarch, no nobility; no nobility, no monarch" ' (SL, 11, 4). I think that we can learn a great deal here from the abstract character of at least a part of Montesquieu's political typology. There is no longer any reason to wait for the *principle* to discover the concrete life of the State: the whole political and *social* order emerges already in its nature.

'These fundamental laws necessarily suppose the intermediate channels through which the power flows' (SL, 11, 4). These 'channels' are precisely the nobility and the clergy. But by a linguistic trick we are again facing a purely legal problem. The 'necessarily' ('these laws *necessarily* appear . . .') is thus really worth its weight in gold. For until now the *necessity* for the nobility and the clergy has not been at all obvious! It is by no means a primordial necessity. It is a necessity in the sense in which we speak of the *necessity one is in* to accept a certain means supposing one wants a particular end. This necessity consists in the fact that *in the absence of intermediate orders there is nothing to prevent the king being a despot*. For, 'in monarchies, the prince is the source of all power, political and civil'; but 'if there be only the momentary and capricious will of a single person to govern the State, nothing can be fixed, and of course there is no fundamental law' (SL, 11, 4). Everything is in these four lines. The fundamental law is the fixity and constancy of a regime. All right. We are in the legal field. But it is *also* the existence of privileged orders. Now we are in the social field. It follows from this reasoning that these orders are identical with the fixity and constancy. The reason for this remarkable identity is that a monarch without a nobility and without orders is not inconceivable, *but he would be despotic*. The performance of the mechanics of power (the *channels*) serves the cause of the orders and combats that of the despot which any prince is if he dispenses with the nobility. Hence we can conclude that in essentials, these fixed and established laws are no more than *the fixity of the establishment of the nobility and the clergy*.

Given this, the juridical argument returns to the fore. And Montesquieu is pleased to describe the *dynamic* peculiar to this regime of intermediary bodies *as if it were a matter of a pure form of the political distribution of power*.

It is very remarkable that the metaphor that haunts despotism is taken from colliding bodies – while the one that haunts monarchy derives from a flowing spring. Water which flows from an elevated spring, passes into channels which moderate its speed and guide its course – and at the bottom reaches the lands which owe it their verdure. The image of colliding balls implies immediacy in time and space, and the 'force' entirely transmitted by the impact. That is why in despotism power is either exercised or handed over. The image of the irrigating spring implies, on the contrary, *space* and *duration*. Its temporality being its course, time is needed for the water to flow. And it never all flows away: a spring does not empty like a basin, it always contains more than it gives away. And contrary to the ball which may be ejected in the opposite direction to the one with which it collided, their instantaneous impact sharply separating them, flowing water never breaks with itself. It is the same uninterrupted stream, from the spring to the most distant lands.

Such is the power of the prince. He never abdicates it, as the despot does, entirely into the hands of a third party. However much power he gives to ministers, governors and captains, he always retains more. And the world in which he exercizes it, its extent, the 'channels' which he has to grant the loan of it, all impose on him a necessary slowness which is the very duration of his power. In fact the nature of monarchical government presupposes a real space and duration. The space: the king does not fill it by himself, in it he meets a social structure which is extended because it is differentiated, composed of orders and estates, each having its *place*. The space which is the measure of the extent of the royal power is thus the limit of his authority. The space is an obstacle. The infinite plain of despotism is a kind of narrow horizon before the despot, precisely because it contains none of those *accidents* constituted by the inequalities of men: it has been levelled. It is the following obstacles: the nobility, the clergy, that give the space its political depth, just as the following obstacles: hedges, roofs and steeples give it its visual depth. And the *time* of the royal power is merely this space *experienced*. As a man endowed with the supreme power, the king is a prey to haste, everything seeming to be a matter of decree. He will learn the *slowness* of the very world he governs, of the privileged orders, and of that body entirely devoted to teaching it him in a good monarchy: *the depository of the laws*. This slowness will be a kind of enforced education of the sovereign's political reason by the real and full distance which separates him from his subjects. It is from this distance that he will acquire reason. This prince, who is certainly no angel, will become reasonable by the very necessity of his power: its space and duration will be the practical reason of a king, forced to become wise by experience, if he is not so by birth. In a democracy the notables, by their rank and fortune, stand in for reason for the people; in the same way, in a monarchy, the nobility stands in for wisdom for the king.

But there is one essential difference between democracy and monarchy. In a democracy it is absolutely necessary that there be virtue and reason *somewhere*, and that *some* men be reasonable of themselves who could not hope to be so despite themselves. It is impossible for a republic to be democratic if its notables are not virtuous. The fate of reason is thus handed over to men themselves, even if it is only delegated to a few of them. It is quite different in a monarchy. The nobility that stands in for wisdom for the king is not forced to be wise. On the contrary, it is its nature to be unreasonable. It is incapable of reflection, so much so that it has to look to lawyers to remember the laws it does not want to forget! Whence then does monarchy, in which nothing is reasonable, derive this reason? From the nobility, which does not have any, but *produces* it without wishing it or realizing it, without even having anything to do with it. It is thus just as if monarchy produced political reason as the result of its private unreasons. This reason, which features under none of the rubrics, is there nonetheless in the whole. It is surely the most profound law of monarchy that it produces its end despite itself in this way. If its fundamental laws need to be complemented by one last one, which is really the first, it would be to state that the original law of monarchy is this *ruse of reason*.

This is what constitutes the very essence of *honour*, the principle of monarchy. Indeed, the truth of honour lies in the fact that it is *false*. 'Philosophically speaking, it is a false honour,' says Montesquieu (SL, III, 7). This falsity has to be understood in two senses. First, that the truth of honour has nothing to do with the truth. Second, that this lie produces a truth in its own despite.

Honour has nothing to do with truth, nor with morality. This seems to clash with all the appearances of honour itself, since honour means frankness, obedience, politeness and generosity. Frankness? For honour, 'truth . . . in conversation, is here a necessary point. But is it for the sake of truth? By no means' (SL, IV, 2). Such a love of 'truth and simplicity' is to be found in the people, who have no part in honour, but not in honour, which is only interested in truth 'because a person habituated to veracity has an air of boldness and freedom'. Obedience? Honour does not accept it for obedience's sake, but for honour's sake, not for the goodness or virtue of submission, but for the grandeur restored to it by the choice it makes to submit. The proof is that this entirely submissive honour subjects the status of the commands it receives to its own judgement: disobeying all those it reckons dishonourable, all those that conflict with its own laws and codes. Politeness and generosity, greatness of soul? These are indeed obligatory duties for all men towards their kind if they are to live together in peace. But in honour 'politeness, generally speaking, does not derive its original from so pure a source: it rises from a desire of distinguishing ourselves. It is pride that renders us polite, we are flattered with being taken notice of for a behaviour that shews we are not of a mean condition, and that we have not been bred up with those who in all ages are considered as the scum of the people' (SL, IV, 2). Generosity itself, which seems to flow from goodness, is merely the proof that a well-born soul wants to present itself as greater than its fortune, by giving it away, and above its rank, by forgetting it; as if it could deny the advantage of rank that is required to have the pleasure of denying it. All the appearances of virtue have thus been turned upside down. For honour is not so much the subject of virtue as its subjugator. 'To this whimsical honour it is owing that the virtues are only just what it pleases: it adds rules of its own invention to every thing prescribed to us: it extends or limits our duties according to its own fancy, whether they proceed from religion, politics, or morality' (SL, IV, 2).

Does honour then have some relation with a different truth that is no longer theoretical or moral, but quite practical and profane? It looks like it when we find Montesquieu seeking in the barbarous laws, which subordinated the judge's decision to trial by *combat*, for the origin of honour in the *point of honour*. This recalls Hobbes and his extraordinary image of the destiny of men in struggle. In the endless race which constitutes our whole life, we are on a kind of track in which we all started together. Until death, which is to abandon the race, we continue to struggle, endlessly trying to pass one another. Honour is then *to turn round and see that there are people behind us*. That is Hobbes's honour, which expresses both the human wish to take advantage of man and the real and conscious merit of having improved on men. But it is not Montesquieu's honour. For him, honour is not the spring of the human condition, the universal passion which arouses the universal struggle for prestige and recognition in which

Hegel was to see the origin of the master and the slave, and of self-consciousness. In Montesquieu, the masters and slaves always pre-exist honour; its triumph never celebrates a real triumph. The race was run before the starter's flag. In honour, if we must still speak of a race, some have twenty years start, as Pascal puts it, and all the race is in the procedure. This is because in fact if honour does demand 'honours and distinctions', it presupposes their sanctioned existence and their regular attribution – in other words, it presupposes a State in which 'pre-eminences and ranks' prevail (SL, III, 7). Honour is the point of honour not of a merit attained in the struggle, but of a superiority obtained by birth. Honour is thus *the passion of a social class*. If it seems to be its father, since it was constituted in the distant origin of barbarous laws, when the Franks defeated the Gauls, its father, since it maintains it in the conviction of its superiority, honour is rather the *child of the nobility*, since outside the existence of the nobility it would be inconceivable. And all its falsity consists in the fact that it gives the appearance of morality or merit to reasons which pertain to the vanity of a class.

But honour is false, not only because of its ruse with truth. It is false because this lie produces a truth. This strange passion, in fact so regulated that its whimsicalities have their laws and a whole code which seems to invert the social order by its contempt for order and society, serves the reason of the State by its very unreason. For honour, with its ruse of truth and morality, is itself the dupe of its own ruse. It thinks it knows no other duty than the duty one recognizes for oneself: the duty to distinguish oneself, to perpetuate one's own grandeur, to care for a certain self-image that raises one above one's own life, and the orders one receives. In fact, 'each individual advances the public good, while he only thinks of promoting his own interest' (SL, III, 7). In fact 'this false honour is as useful to the public as a true honour could possibly be to private people' (ibid.). The virtues, false in their cause, are true in their effects: obedience, frankness, politeness and generosity. What does it matter to the prince whether he obtains them from morality and truth, or from vanity

and prejudice? Their effect is the same, and without the super-
human effort required of virtue in the same cause. Honour is the
economy of virtue. It dispenses with it and gives the same effects
at a lower cost.

But there is a quite different merit, one which is of concern
precisely to the prince who keeps the accounts and takes the
profits: it will not let itself be beaten by anything, not even by the
prestige of the supreme power. That it is above any laws, not just
religious and moral ones, but also political ones, means that
honour is the rock against the king's fancies. If the power of
honour is 'limited by its very spring' (SL, III, 10), if the great
only ever have honour on their minds, this sufficiency suffices
them. They have no other ambition at heart, whether of fortunes
to be won or of power to be conquered; if honour is this blinding
of the great to the real interests of the world, if its folly thus
protects the prince from their audacity as the great, this folly also
protects the prince against his own temptations as a man. For he
can never hope that these great ones will ever enter into his plans
for other reasons than their own, for motives foreign to this
strange honour. He may lay claim to their complete service, but
never their entire soul. And if he tries to go beyond reason and
throw himself into enterprises which exceed the legitimate power,
he will be held back by the honour of his nobles, which will
oppose his laws to his orders and make the latter rebels. That is
how reason will reign in the State, as the powerlessness of two
follies, and truth, as two contradictory falsities. We can tell from
this trait whether honour does not as the *principle* in this government play the same part as the nobility and the intermediary
bodies do as the *nature*. And whether honour, far from being a
general passion, as virtue must be in a republic, is not the passion
of an *estate*, which may be contagious, as examples always are,
but cannot be shared. Hidden away in a chapter on penal law we
can read a short sentence to the effect that 'the peasant . . . has no
honour to lose' (SL, VI, 10). Which makes him worthy to suffer
bodily the punishments for his crimes. A great man is tortured in his
honour, which is his soul. Shame thus taking the place of the wheel.

Such is monarchy. A prince protected from his own excesses by privileged orders. Orders protected from the prince by their honour. A prince protected from the people and a people protected from the prince by these same orders. Everything depending on the nobility. A power moderated less by its pure essence or its attribution than by the fixed and established social conditions in which it is exercized, and which, as obstacle and means, give it the slowness and conciliation which are its entire rationale. Each individual pulling for himself, having his own absolute in his head, and the equilibrium emerging, as if unbeknownst to all, from these very contradictory excesses. The reason of monarchy may well be described as a contrariety of follies. And as it is clear that this order is the one Montesquieu prefers, its structure may cast light on certain of his choices. And especially the ideas he has of men and reason. For if he does possess a true enthusiasm for intelligent reason, he has no passion for ideal reason. Montesquieu occasionally says that the reasonable is not all of reason, and that to do well is not to do good. If he holds republican virtue so high, it is because he believes that it is always more or less angelic and out of human reach. If he prefers to it the conciliation of monarchy and honour, it is indeed because honour, in its round-about way, is the short-cut to virtue, but above all because this short-cut is made via passions born from the nature of a condition and not by the asceticism of a conversion. This reason he dreams of making supreme in the State is far rather the reason which acts behind men's backs and on them than the reason that lives in their consciousness, and by which they live. It is clear how monarchy naturally enters into that great law of history, already discovered, that it is not the consciousness of men that makes history. But it is also clear how such a general idea can serve such a particular cause. For of all the political unconsciousnesses, it is no mystery to say that Montesquieu knew how to choose the right one: monarchy.

3. DESPOTISM

In the order of Montesquieu's definitions, despotism is the last of the governments. I hope to show that it is the first in his mind. Not according to his preference, which obviously goes to monarchy, but, what comes to the same thing, in his aversion. And that his object is to provide new arguments not only for choosing monarchy, but also for *re-establishing* it on its true foundations, by counterposing to it the spectacle of its downfall and bugbear.

What is despotism? Unlike the republic and like monarchy, it is an *existing* government. It is the government of the Turks, of the Persians, of Japan, of China and of most Asian countries. The government of immense countries with a voracious climate. The location of the despotic regimes already suggests their excess. Despotism is the government of extreme lands, of extreme extents beneath the most ardent skies. It is the limit government, and already the limit of government. It is easy to guess that the example of real countries is only providing Montesquieu with a pretext. Apparently, at the time of the 1948 conference, Turkish listeners, on mention of the famous statement that despotism is the government of the Turks, uttered 'the most lively and most justifiable of protestations'.[3] M. Prélot has gravely related this incident. But without being a Turk, one can suspect the political exoticism of a man who never went beyond Venice and the frontiers of Austria, and only knew the Orient by accounts among which he knew precisely the ones to choose. By 1778, in an admirable work on *Législation orientale*, Anquetil-Duperron was already opposing the real East to Montesquieu's oriental myth. But once the geographical myth of despotism has been denounced, there remains an *idea of despotism* that no Turkish protestation can refute. If the Persian does not exist, where does a French *gentilhomme*, born under Louis XIV, get the *idea* of him?

3. M. Prélot, 'Montesquieu et les formes de gouvernement', in *Receuil Sirey du bicentenaire de l'Esprit des Lois*, p. 127.

Despotism is certainly a political *idea*, the idea of absolute evil, the idea of the very limits of politics as such.

It is in fact insufficient to define despotism as the government 'in which a single person, with neither rules nor laws, directs everything by his own will and caprice'. For this definition remains a superficial one so long as the *concrete* life of such a regime has not been represented. How indeed could *a single person* really direct by his own caprice the immense empire of lands and peoples subject to his decree? This is the paradox that must be illuminated to discover the meaning of the idea.

The first feature of despotism is the fact that it is a political regime which has so to speak *no structure*. Neither legal-political nor social. Montesquieu repeats several times that despotism *has no laws*, and by that we should understand first of all *no fundamental laws*. I know that Montesquieu cites one when he argues that the tyrant delegates all his power to the grand vizir (SL, II, 5), but this only has the appearance of a *political* law. In fact it is simply a law of passion, a psychological law which betrays the bestiality of the tyrant and the divine surprise which reveals to him, in the depths of his laziness, like the Pope Montesquieu cites who resigned the administration of his States to his nephew (ibid.), that the government of men is the art of a child: it is enough to let a third party govern them! In its pretension, this false law, which illegitimately converts passion into politics, suggests that *in despotism all politics can always be reduced entirely to passion*. We still have no structure. I know that there is nonetheless in despotism a substitute for a fundamental law: religion. It is indeed the only authority which is above authority, and can, in some circumstances, moderate the excesses of the prince's cruelty and the subjects' fear. But its essence, too, is passionate, since in despotism religion is itself despotic: 'it is fear added to fear' (SL, V, 14).

Hence neither in the vizirate nor in religion is there anything like an order of political and legal conditions transcending human passions. And in fact despotism knows no laws of succession. Nothing that designates tomorrow's despot to yesterday's subjects. Not even the arbitrary decree of the despot, which can be reduced to nothing by a palace revolution, a harem conspiracy or a popular rising. Nor does it know *political* laws other than the one that governs the strange transmission of power, always absolute, which descends from the prince to the last family head in the land, via the first vizir, the governors, the bashaws, repeating imperturbably from one end of the kingdom to the other the logic of passion: laziness on the one hand, delight in domination on the other. Nor does it know any *judiciary* laws. The only code of the cadi is his humour, the only procedure, his impatience. Hardly has he lent his ear to the parties than he decides, and distributes bastinados or chops off heads on the spot. Lastly, this strange regime does not even bother with that minimum of police that might regulate exchange and commerce. The 'society of needs' is not even governed by the unconscious laws which constitute a market, an economic order transcending the practical life of men: no, the logic of the economy is the economy of logic, it reduces itself to the pure passions of men. The merchant himself lives *from one day to the next* for fear of losing tomorrow whatever surplus he might amass today, in his own way like the American savage cited by Rousseau who in the morning sells the bed he has just left, not thinking that there will be another night this evening. . . . Without political or legal transcendence, i.e. without past or future, despotism is the regime of the moment.

This precariousness is, if I may say so, ensured by the disappearance of any *social structure*. In a democracy, the magistrates have a statute, and property and even relative wealth are guaranteed by the law. In a monarchy, the nobility and the clergy are protected by the recognition of their privileges. In a despotism, nothing distinguishes between men: it is the realm of *extreme equality* which lowers all subjects to the same *uniformity* (SL, V, 14). Here, says Montesquieu, all men are equal, not because they are everything, as in a democracy, but 'because they are nothing' (SL, VI, 2). It is the suppression of orders by a general levelling down. No hereditary order, no nobility: this sanguinary regime cannot tolerate greatness in blood. Nor greatness in goods: the tyrant cannot suffer the continuity of 'families' that time enriches and the succession and effort of generations elevate in human society. Better, he cannot tolerate any of the greatnesses of establishment that he himself confers on certain of his subjects. For ultimately a vizir, governors, bashaws and cadis are needed! But this greatness is only occasional, taken back the moment it is conceded, almost evanescent. It is nothing the moment it has arrived. Every clerk may thus hold all the power of the despot, but his life is a postponed disgrace or assassination: that is all his freedom, that is all his security! It is as easy, says Montesquieu, to make of a prince a scullion, and of a scullion a prince (SL, V, 19). The social distinctions that emerge from this egalitarian desert are no more than the appearance of a universal distinction. But even that body, so necessary to order or terror, the army, has no place in this regime: it would constitute too stable a body, and be too dangerous to the general instability. At most all that is needed is a guard of janissaries attached to the person of the prince, and which he sends out in lightning raids on someone's head, before locking it back up again in the night of the palace. Nothing that distinguishes between men, nothing that resembles in the slightest the outline of a social hierarchy or a social career, the organization of a social world, in which, in advance of and for all the time of the existence and for the growth of the generations, avenues open into the future – in which one may be sure of being noble for life if one is so by birth, of becoming bourgeois in life if one has deserved it by one's industry. No more than it knows any political and legal structure and transcendence, does despotism know any *social structure*.

This disposition gives a strange pace to the life of this regime. This government which reigns over vast spaces in some sense lacks any *social space*. This regime, which has lasted millennia in the Chinese example, is somehow stripped of all *duration*. Its social space and its political time are neutral and uniform. Space without places, time without duration. Kings, says Montesquieu, know the *differences* there are between provinces, and respect them. Despots not only do not know such differences, they destroy them. They reign only over empty uniformity, over the void constituted by the uncertainty of tomorrow, abandoned lands and a commerce that expires at its birth: over *deserts*. And it is the desert itself that despotism establishes at its frontiers, burning lands, even its own, to isolate itself from the world, to protect itself from the contagions and invasions from which nothing else can save it (SL, IX, 4 & 6). In fact, nothing that resists in the void: let a foreign army penetrate into the empire and nothing will stop it, neither strongpoint nor force, since there are none; it is thus necessary to weaken it before it ever reaches the frontier by opposing it with a first desert in which it will perish. The space of despotism is no more than the void: thinking he is governing an empire, the despot reigns only over a desert.

As for the *time* of despotism, it is the opposite of duration: the moment. Not only does despotism know no institutions, no orders and no families that *last*, but also its very own acts spurt out *in a moment*. The entire people is made in the image of the despot. The despot decides in a moment. Without reflecting, without comparing reasons, without weighing arguments, without 'mediums' or 'limitations' (SL, III, 10). For it takes time to reflect, and a certain idea of the future. But the despot has no more idea of the future than the merchant who profits in order to eat and that is all. All his reflection comes down to deciding, and the legion of his precarious administrators *repeat* the same blind gesture to the end of the most remote province. What could they decide anyway? They are like judges without codes. They do not know the tyrant's reasons; he has none anyway. They have to decide! Hence they will follow his 'subitaneous manner of willing' (SL, V, 16). As 'subitaneously' as they will be disgraced or butchered. Sharing in every respect the condition of their master, who would only learn of his future from his death, if he were not dying.

This logic of abstract immediacy, which contains extraordinary inklings of some of Hegel's critical themes, does nonetheless have a certain truth and content. For this regime that survives so to speak *beneath the political and the social*, restricted to the step below their generality and constancy, does at least live the lower life of this step. And this life is solely the life of *immediate* passion.

Perhaps it has not been sufficiently realized that the famous passions that constitute the *principles* of the different governments are not all of the same essence. Honour, for example, is not a simple passion, or, if you prefer, is not a 'psychological' passion. Honour is capricious like all passions, but its caprices are *regulated*: it has its laws and its code. It would not require much pressure to make Montesquieu admit that the essence of monarchy is a disobedience, but a *regulated* disobedience. Honour is thus a reflected passion, even in its own intransigence. However 'psychological', however immediate, honour is a passion highly educated by society, a cultivated passion, and, if the term can be suggested, a *cultural and social* passion.

The same is true of the passion of the republic. It, too, is a strange passion, one which has nothing immediate about it but sacrifices in man his own wishes to give him the general good as his object. Virtue is defined as the passion for the general. And Montesquieu obligingly shows us certain monks shifting to the generality of their order all the ardour of the particular passions they repress in themselves. Like honour, virtue thus has its code and its laws. Or rather it has *its law*, a single law: love of the fatherland. This passion for universality demands a universal education: the school of all life itself. Montesquieu answered the old Socratic question – can virtue educate itself? – by saying, it must, and the whole destiny of virtue is precisely to be taught.

The passion that sustains despotism knows not this duty. Fear,[4] since it must be called by its name, needs no education, and the latter is, in despotism, 'in some measure, needless' (SL, IV, 3). It is not a compound or educated passion, nor a social passion. It knows neither codes nor laws. It is a passion without a career before it, and with no title behind it: a passion *in statu nascendi* which nothing will ever divert from its birth. A momentary

4. It is very remarkable that Montesquieu reserves fear, which Hobbes, the theorist of absolutism, found at the heart of all societies, to despotism alone.

passion which only ever repeats itself. Among the *political* passions it is the only one which is not political, but 'psychological', because immediate. Nonetheless, this is the passion that constitutes the life of this strange regime.

If the tyrant resigns the exercise of government out of laziness and boredom, that is because he refuses to be a public man. It is because he does not want to pretend to that order of considered impersonality which constitutes a statesman. By a movement of private whim or lassitude, which dresses up in the trappings of solemnity, he divests himself of the public personage and hands it over to a third party, as a king hands his cloak to a valet, in order to abandon himself to the delights of private passions. The despot is no more than his desires. Hence the harem. *This abdication of the despot is the general form of the regime that renounces the order of the political in order to give itself up to the destiny of the passions alone.* It is hardly surprising therefore to see the same pattern repeated indefinitely in all the men making up the empire. The lowliest subject is a despot, at least over his wives, but also their prisoner: the prisoner of his passions. When he leaves his house, it is his desires that move him once more. This shows that in a despotism, the only desire that survives is a desire for the 'conveniences of life'.[5] But this is not a desire followed through: it does not have the time to compose itself a future. Thus the passions of despotism overturn into one another. The spring of despotism could be said to be desire as much as fear. For they are for themselves their own inverses, without any future, like two men tied back to back with no space between them, riveted to the spot by their chains. And it is this model of passion that gives despotism its style. That absence of duration, those sudden, irretrievable movements are precisely the attributes of these momentary and immediate passions which fall back on themselves like stones children hope to throw to heaven. If it is true, as Marx said in a youthful image, that politics is the heaven of private men, despotism can be described as a world without a heaven.

5. SL, V, 17 & 18; VII, 4. Cf. IX, 6: Despotism is the reign of 'private interest'.

It is only too clear that what Montesquieu has been trying to represent in this picture of despotism is something quite different from the State in oriental regimes: it is *the abdication of politics itself*. This value-judgement explains its paradoxical character. In fact, despotism is always on the brink of being considered as a regime *which does not exist* but is the temptation and peril of the other regimes when corrupted; and yet as a regime *which does exist*, and can even *be corrupted;* although corrupt in essence, it can never fall into anything but corruption itself. No doubt that is the fate of all reprobate extremes: it is convenient to represent them as real in order to inspire disgust. It takes many pictures of the devil to uphold virtue. But it·is also important to give the extremity all the features of the impossible and of negativity; to show that it is not what it claims; and to destroy in it even the appearances of the good that would be lost if one lapsed into it. That is why the image of despotism is justified by the example of the regimes of the East, at a time when the latter impressed itself and was refuted as an *idea*. Let us therefore leave the Turks and the Chinese in peace, and focus on the positive image for which this danger is the bugbear.

We have a sufficient number of texts and sufficiently categorical ones by Montesquieu and his contemporaries to suggest that despotism is only a geographical illusion because it is a historical allusion. It is *absolute monarchy* that is Montesquieu's target, or if not absolute monarchy in person, then at least the temptations to which it is prone.[6] As is well known, Montesquieu belonged by conviction to that right-wing oppositional party of feudal extraction which did not accept the political decline of its class and attacked the new political forms inaugurated since the fourteenth century for having supplanted the older ones. Fénelon, Boulainvilliers and Saint-Simon were of this party, which, until his death, set all its hopes on the Duc de Bourgogne, whom

6. Cf. the 37th Persian letter: A Portrait of Louis XIV. Usbeck: 'He hath often been heard to say, that of all the governments in the world, that of the Turks, or of our august Sultan, pleased him best; so highly does he esteem the politics of the East.'

Montesquieu made his hero.[7] It is to this party that we owe the most famous of the *doléances* against the excesses of Louis XIV's reign. The poverty of the peasantry, the horrors of war, the intrigues and usurpations of courtesans, these are the themes of its denunciations. All these famous texts acquired 'liberal' overtones by their oppositional character, and I am afraid that they often feature in anthologies of '*la liberté*' alongside those of Montesquieu himself, and not without a well-established appearance of correctness, for this opposition took a unique part in the struggle against the feudal power really, and whatever they may have said, embodied by the absolute monarchy; but the purposes which inspired them had about as much relation to liberty as the ultras' clamour against capitalist society under the Restoration and the July Monarchy had with socialism. In denouncing 'despotism', Montesquieu is not defending against the politics of absolutism so much *liberty in general* as the *particular liberties* of the feudal class, its individual security, the conditions of its lasting survival and its pretensions to return in new organs of power to the place which had been robbed from it by history.

No doubt 'despotism' is a caricature. But its object is to terrify and to edify by its very horribleness. Here is a regime in which a single individual governs, in a palace he never leaves, prey to feminine passions and the intrigues of courtesans. A caricature of Versailles and the Court. Here is a tyrant who governs through his grand vizir. A caricature of the minister[8] whom nothing, above all not his birth, entitles to that post save the prince's

7. 'The death of the last dauphin was a dreadful wound for the kingdom. . . . Although all the diverse plans for his government were unknown, it is still certain that he had the grandest ideas in the world. It is certain that there was nothing in the world he hated so much as despotism. He wanted to restore all the various provinces of the kingdom their Estates, like Breton and Languedoc. He proposed that there should be councils and that State secretaries should only be the secretaries of these councils. He proposed to reduce the costs of office (*charges de la robe*) to the necessary level. He proposed that the King have a kind of civil list as in England, for the upkeep of his house and court, and that in time of war this civil list should be taxed like other funds, for, he said, it is unjust that all the subjects should suffer from the war without the prince suffering too. He proposed that his court should have some morals' (*Spicilège*, p. 767, Pléiade edition, op. cit., vol. II, pp. 1429–30).

8. 'The two worst citizens France has known: Richelieu and Louvois' (*Mes Pensées*, Pléiade edition, op. cit., vol. I, p. 1120).

favour. And even in the all-powerful governors dispatched to the provinces, can we fail to recognize the grotesque masks of the intendants charged with the King's omnipotence in their domains? How could we fail to suspect in the regime of caprice a forced caricature of the regime of *'bon plaisir'*, in the tyrant who is *'tout l'État'* without saying it, a distorted echo of the Prince who had already said it, even if it was not yet completely true. But a cause has to be judged by its effects. Once we see the respective situations of the *great* and the *people* in despotism, we will realize the dangers against which it was meant to be a forewarning.

The paradox of despotism is to make such an effective attack on the *great*, whatever their extraction (and how could we fail to think of the nobility, the least revocable of the great?),[9] that the people are in some sense spared. The despot has so much to do to defeat the great and destroy the threat of the rebirth of their condition, that the people, who know nothing of such things, are sheltered from this struggle unleashed over their heads. In a certain sense, despotism is the great brought down and the people tranquil in their passions and affairs. Sometimes, says Montesquieu, one sees torrents swollen by storms descend the mountain, ravaging all in their paths. But all around there are only green fields and grazing flocks. In the same way, despots sweep away the great, while the people, though poverty-stricken, know a kind of peace. I admit that this is only a 'tranquillity' and indeed the tranquillity that reigns in a besieged town, since it is in these terms that Montesquieu criticizes it (SL, V, 14), but who would not prefer it to the terror of the great, who live in the 'pallor' of expected blows, if not death? When we come upon these passages, which Montesquieu almost seems to let slip (SL, XIII, 12, 15 & 19; III, 9), it is clear that inadvertance has nothing to do with it. It is in fact a *warning* which has also the meaning of a reminder. The lesson is clear: the *great* have everything to fear from despotism, from terror to destruction. The people, however miserable they may be, are protected.

9. 'As the instability of the great is natural to a despotic government, so their security is interwoven with the nature of monarchy' (SL, VI, 21).

Protected. But also just as threatening in their own way. For despotism presents a second privilege: that it is *the regime of popular revolution*.[10] No other government leaves the people to their passions alone, and God knows, the people are subject to them! These popular passions need the bridle of reflection: the notables elected in a republic; the intermediary bodies found in a monarchy. But in a despotism, in which passion reigns supreme, how are the people's instincts to be chained, in the absence of any order, legal or social, which they will accept? When passions dominate, the people, who are passion, always win in the end. Even if only for a day. But this day is enough to destroy everything. Enough at any rate to overthrow the tyrant in the shocks of a revolution. All this is plain to read in Book V, Chapter 11 of the *Spirit of Laws*.[11] And it is hard to avoid drawing a *second lesson*, this time not addressed to the *great*, but to the *tyrants*, or by extension *to those modern monarchs tempted by despotism*. This second lesson clearly signifies: despotism is the sure road to popular revolutions. *Princes, avoid despotism if you would save your thrones from the people's violence!*

10. SL, V, 11; cf. VI, 2: In a despotism 'everything leads to sudden and unforseen revolutions'.

11. SL, V, 11: 'Monarchy has a great advantage over a despotic government. As it naturally requires there should be several orders or ranks of subjects, the State is more permanent, the constitution more steady, and the person of him who governs more secure.

'Cicero is of the opinion that the establishing of the tribunes preserved the republic. "And, indeed (says he), the violence of a heedless people is more terrible. A chief, or head, is sensible that the affair depends upon himself, and therefore he thinks; but the people, in their impetuosity, are ignorant of the danger into which they hurry themselves." This reflection may be applied to a despotic government, which is a people without tribunes, and to a monarchy, where the people have some sort of tribunes.

'Accordingly, it is observable, that, in the commotions of a despotic government, the people, hurried away by their passions, are apt to push things as far as they can go. The disorders they commit are all extreme; whereas, in monarchies, matters are seldom carried to excess. The chiefs are apprehensive on their own account; they are afraid of being abandoned; and the intermediate dependent powers do not choose that the populace should have too much the upper hand. . . .

'Thus all our histories are full of civil wars without revolutions, while the histories of despotic governments abound with revolutions without civil wars. . . .

'Monarchs, who live under the fundamental laws of their country, are far happier than despotic princes, who have nothing to regulate either their own passions or those of their subjects.'

These two lessons together constitute *a third:* if the prince ruthlessly fights the *great*, the great will thereby lose their conditions of existence. But in doing so, the prince will have cleared the way for the people, who will turn against him, and nothing now protects him from their blows: he will thereby lose his crown and his life. *Hence let the prince understand that he needs the rampart provided by the great to defend his crown and his life against the people!* That is the basis for a fine and completely reasonable alliance based on mutual advantage. All he has to do to secure his throne is to recognize the nobility.

Such is despotism. An *existing regime*, certainly, but also and above all an *existing threat* which hangs over the other regime of the present day, monarchy. An existing regime, certainly, but also and above all a political lesson, a clear warning to a king tempted by absolute power. It is clear that despite its apparent detachment, the original list conceals a secret choice. Maybe there are *three species of government*. But one, the republic, does not exist except in historical memory. We are left with monarchy and despotism. But despotism is no more than abusive, perverted monarchy. We are thus left with monarchy alone, a monarchy to be protected from its perils. So much for the *present period*.

But, it will be said, what of the *future?* And what about the *English Constitution* which Montesquieu presents as an ideal in the famous sixth chapter of Book xi? Is it not a new model, superseding all the earlier lessons? I hope to prove that it is nothing of the kind, and that the logic of the theory of monarchy and despotism constitutes if not all the meanings, at least one important one, of the famous debate about the *separation of powers*.

Chapter Five

The Myth of the
Separation of Powers

This is a famous text. Who is not familiar with the theory according to which every good government rigorously distinguishes between the *legislature*, the *executive* and the *judiciary*? That it guarantees the *independence* of each of these powers in order to obtain from this *separation* the advantages of *moderation*, *security* and *liberty*? Such, according to this theory, is in fact the secret of Book XI, conceived later than the first ten, and inspired in Montesquieu by the revelation of England, where, during a stay in 1729–30, he discovered a radically new regime with no other object than *liberty*. Before Book XI, Montesquieu presented a *classical* theory, distinguishing different political forms, describing their peculiar economies and dynamics. He then threw off the mask of the dispassionate historian, and even, if it is to be believed, that of the partisan *gentilhomme*, to give the public the ideal of a nation with two chambers, an assembly of the third estate, and elected judges. Thereby, for some, Montesquieu at last reached the sphere of the political as such, and demonstrated his genius in a theory of the balance of the powers, so well arranged that power is itself the limit of power, thus resolving once and for all *the* political problem, which is entirely a matter of the *use* and *abuse* of power; for others, the political problems of the *future*,[1] which are less those of monarchy in general than those of representative and parliamentary government. The temporal succession is in some sense the guarantee of this interpretation. Did not the age as a whole look to Montesquieu for arguments to weaken

1. Prélot, op. cit., pp. 123, 129ff.

the monarchical order, to justify parliaments, and even for the convocation of the Estates General? Did not the American Constitution of the end of the century and the French Constitution of 1791 itself, not to speak of those of 1795 and 1848, consecrate Montesquieu's desired principles of the separation of powers in their arguments and dispositions? These two themes: the separation of powers, the balance of powers, are they not still current themes, still taken up and disputed in the very words established by Montesquieu?

I hope to be able to argue that this is almost completely a historical illusion, and give reasons for it. In this vein, I should first like to make explicit all I owe the articles of the jurist *Charles Eisenmann*.[2] I should like to repeat the essential points of these articles here before extending their conclusions.

Eisenmann's thesis is that Montesquieu's theory, and in particular the famous chapter on the Constitution of England, has produced a real *myth*: the *myth of the separation of powers*. A whole school of jurists arose, particularly at the end of the nineteenth and the beginning of the twentieth century, which took advantage of a number of isolated formulations of Montesquieu's in order to impose on him a *purely imaginary* theoretical model. According to this model, Montesquieu's political ideal coincides with a regime in which this *separation of powers* is rigorously guaranteed. There should be three powers: the executive (the king, his ministers), the legislature (the lower and upper chambers) and the judiciary (the body of magistrates). Each power corresponds precisely to its own sphere, i.e. its own function, without any interference. Each power in each sphere is provided for by an organ rigorously distinct from the other organs. Not only can there be no encroachment of the executive onto the legislature or judiciary, or any reciprocal encroachment of the same kind; but also none of the parts constituting an organ can belong to any other organ. For example, not only can the executive not inter-

2. See in particular: Eisenmann, 'L'Esprit des Lois et la séparation des pouvoirs', *Mélanges Carré de Malberg*, Paris 1933, pp. 163–92; 'La pensée constitutionnelle de Montesquieu,' *Recueil Sirey*, op. cit., pp. 133–60.

vene in the legislature by proposing laws or in the judiciary by pressure, etc., not only can no minister be responsible to the legislature, but also no member of the legislature can, in his personal capacity, assume executive and judicial functions, i.e. become a minister or a magistrate, etc. I leave aside the details of this logic, which is still alive in some people's minds.

Eisenmann's first audacity was to show that this famous theory *quite simply does not exist in Montesquieu*. A careful reading of his texts shows, in fact:

1. That the executive encroaches on the legislature, since the king has the *power of veto*.[3]

2. That the legislature can to a certain extent exercize a right of inspection over the executive, since it checks on the application of the laws it has voted, and, without there being any question of 'ministerial responsibility' to parliament, can ask for accounts from the ministers.[4]

3. That the legislature encroaches seriously on the judiciary, since, in three special circumstances, it sets itself up as a tribunal: in all matters, the nobles, whose dignity must be preserved from any contact with the prejudices of popular magistrates, will be judged by their peers in the upper chamber;[5] in questions of amnesty;[6] and in questions of political trials, which are brought before the tribunal of the upper chamber on the impeachment of the lower chamber.[7]

3. 'The executive power has no other part in the legislative than the power of rejecting' (SL, XI, 6).
4. The legislative power 'has a right, and ought to have the means, of examining in what manner its laws have been executed'; the ministers must give an 'account of their administration' (SL, XI, 6).
5. 'The great are always obnoxious to popular envy: and, were they to be judged by the people, they might be in danger from their judges, and would moreover be deprived of the privilege, which the meanest subject is possessed of in a free State, of being tried by his peers. The nobility, for this reason, ought not to be cited before the ordinary courts of the judicature, but before that part of the legislature which is compounded of their own body' (SL, XI, 6).
6. 'It is possible that the law . . . might, in some cases, be too severe. . . . That part . . . of the legislative body, which we have just now observed to be a necessary tribunal on another occasion, is also a necessary tribunal in this: it belongs to its supreme authority to moderate the law in favour of the law itself' (SL, XI, 6).
7. 'It might also happen, that a subject, intrusted with the administration of

It is hard to see how such important interferences of powers as these can be reconciled with the claimed purity of their *separation*.

Eisenmann's second audacity was to show that in fact Montesquieu is not concerned about the *separation*, but about the *combination*, *fusion* and *liaison* of these powers.[8] The essential point of this proof consists first of being clear that the judicial power is not a power in the true sense of the word. This power is 'in some measure, next to nothing', says Montesquieu.[9] And in fact, for him the judge is only a sight and a voice. It is a man whose only function is to read and speak the law.[10] This interpretation is disputable, but it must at least be admitted that in matters where the judge threatened to be more than an animated code, Montesquieu was careful to enact guarantees which are no longer legal but *political*: for example, look who judges the crimes and delictions of the nobles and political cases! Once taken, these precautions which transfer any political effects the judiciary may have to more strictly political organs ensure that the rest of the judiciary really is 'next to nothing'. We then confront *two powers*: the executive and the legislature. Two *pouvoirs* but three *puissances*, to use Montesquieu's own words.[11] These three

public affairs, may infringe the rights of the people. . . . In general, the legislative power cannot try causes; and much less can it try this particular case, where it represents the party aggrieved, which is the people. It can only, therefore, impeach. But before what court shall it bring its impeachment? Must it go and demean itself before the ordinary tribunals, which are its inferiors, and, being composed moreover of men who are chosen from the people as well as itself, will naturally be swayed by the authority of so powerful an accuser? No: in order to preserve the dignity of the people and the security of the subject, the legislative part which represents the people must bring in its charge before the legislative part which represents the nobility, who have neither the same interests nor the same passions' (SL, XI, 6).

8. 'The legislative body being composed of two parts, they check one another. . . . They are both restrained by the executive power, as the executive is by the legislative' (SL, XI, 6). 'The three powers are . . . distributed and founded' (SL, XI, 7).

9. 'Of the three powers above-mentioned, the judiciary is, in some sense, next to nothing' (SL, XI, 6).

10. 'The national judges are no more than the mouth that pronounces the words of the law, mere passive beings, incapable of moderating either its force or rigour' (SL, XI, 6).

11. Cf. the passage on Venice in S L, X I, 6: 'Thus at Venice, the legislative power (*pouvoir*) is in the *council*, the executive in the *pregadi*, and the judiciary in the *quarantia*. But the mischief is, that these different tribunals are composed of magis-

puissances are the king, the upper chamber and the lower chamber, i.e. the king, the nobility and the 'people'. Here Eisenmann shows very convincingly that Montesquieu's true object is precisely the *combination*, the *liaison* of these three *puissances*.[12] That what is involved is above all a *political* problem of relations of forces, not a *juridical* problem concerning the definition of legality and its spheres.

This casts light on the famous problem of *moderate* government. True moderation is neither the strict separation of *powers* (pouvoirs) nor a *juridical* concern and respect for legality. At Venice, for example, there are indeed three powers and three distinct organs: but the 'mischief' is that these three organs 'are composed of magistrates all belonging to the same body; which constitutes almost one and the same *puissance*' (SL, XI, 6). Thus it is all very well to say that despotism is the regime in which a single person governs alone, without rules or laws, or that the despot appears in every prince or minister who goes beyond the law and abuses his power. At bottom, this is not what is at issue, for we are familiar with regimes in which despotism reigns even under the appearance of laws, and, says, Montesquieu, that is the worst of tyrannies.[13] *Moderation* is something quite different: it is not mere respect for legality, it is the balance of powers, i.e. *the division of the pouvoirs among the puissances*, and the limitation or moderation of the pretensions of one *puissance* by the *pouvoir* of the others. The famous *separation of powers* is thus no more than the calculated division of *pouvoir* between determinate *puissances:* the king, the nobility and the 'people'.

I think that my remarks on despotism make it possible to go beyond these pertinent conclusions. For this illumination itself poses a question: *to whose advantage is the division made?* If we

trates all belonging to the same body; which constitutes almost one and the same power (*puissance*).'

12. Eisenmann, 'La pensée constitutionnelle de Montesquieu,' op. cit., pp. 154ff.

13. 'No tyranny can have a severer effect than that which is exercised under the appearance of laws, and with the plausible colours of justice' (*Considerations . . .* , Ch. XIV).

were satisfied at having revealed beneath the mythical exterior of the *separation of powers* the real operation of a division of power between different political forces, we would risk encouraging the illusion of a *natural* division, one that occurs of itself and answers to an obvious equity. We have moved from powers to *puissances*. The terms have changed? The problem remains the same: it is never more than a question of balance and division. This is the last myth I hope to be able to expose.

We can illuminate the meaning of this division and its ulterior motives, given of course that Montesquieu is concerned with the *combination of puissances* and not with the *separation of powers*, by *examining all the possible encroachments of one power on another and all the possible combinations of one power with another, in order to find which encroachments and combinations are absolutely excluded.* I have found two, which are of prime importance.

The first *excluded combination* is for the legislature to usurp the powers of the executive: which would immediately consummate the collapse of monarchy into popular despotism.[14] But the *inverse is not the case*. Montesquieu accepts that monarchy may survive and even retain its *moderation*, if the king controls not only the executive, but also the legislative power.[15] But let the people become the prince and all will be lost.

The second *excluded combination* is more famous, but to my mind it has been treated as too obvious and for that reason not fully examined. It concerns the investment of the judiciary in the executive, the king. Montesquieu is strict: *this arrangement is enough to bring about a collapse of monarchy into despotism.* If the king himself judged, 'the constitution by such means would be

14. 'Should the legislative power (*puissance*) usurp a share of the executive, the latter would be . . . undone' (SL, XI, 6).

'If there were no monarch, and the executive power (*puissance*) should be committed to a certain number of persons, selected from the legislative body, there would be an end of liberty' (ibid.).

15. 'In modern monarchies, the prince is invested with the executive and legislative powers (*puissances*), or, at least, with a part of the legislative, but does not act in a judiciary capacity' (SL, XI, 11).

'Most kingdoms in Europe enjoy a moderate government, because the prince, who is invested with the two first powers (*pouvoirs*), leaves the third to his subjects' (SL, XI, 6).

subverted, and the dependent intermediate powers annihilated' (SL, VI, 5), and the example he cites in the following pages is that of Louis XIII, who wanted to judge a gentleman himself (ibid.). If we compare this exclusion and the arguments for it (that if the king judges, the intermediate bodies are annihilated) on the one hand with the arrangement that only calls noblemen before a tribunal of their peers, and on the other with the misfortunes the despot reserves primarily for the *great*, we can see that *this special clause depriving the king of judiciary power is important above all for the protection of the nobility* against the political and legal arbitration of the prince, and that once again the despotism Montesquieu threatens us with designates a policy directed quite precisely *against the nobility* first of all.

If we now return to the famous balance of the *puissances*, we can, I think, propose an answer to the question: *to whose advantage does the division work?* If we stop considering the forces invoked in Montesquieu's combination and look at the really existing forces of his day, we have to state that *the nobility gains two considerable advantages from his project*: as a class, it becomes directly a political force recognized in the upper chamber; also, by the clause which excludes royal power from the exercise of judgement and also by that other clause which reserves this power to the upper chamber, where the nobility is concerned, it becomes a class whose members' prospects, social position, privileges and distinctions are guaranteed *against the undertakings of either the king or the people*. As a result, in their lives, their families and their wealth, the nobility are safe both from the king and from the people. How better to guarantee the conditions for the permanent survival of a decadent class, whose ancient prerogatives are being torn from it and disputed by history?

The counterpart to these assurances is another assurance, but this time one *for the king's benefit*. The assurance that the monarch will be protected by *the social and political rampart of the nobility* against popular revolutions. The assurance that he will not find himself in the situation of the despot, abandoned and alone face to face with his people and his passions. If he is prepared to learn the lesson of despotism, the king will realize that *his future is well worth a nobility*.

Not only will this nobility serve as a counter-weight to the 'people', since, with a representation out of proportion to the numbers and interests of the masses, it will balance the representation of the people in the legislature, but also by its existence, its privileges, its lustre and its luxury, even by its generosity, this nobility will teach the people in concrete daily life that greatness is respect-worthy, that there is a structure to the State, that it is far from the passion for power, that in the moderate space of a monarchy the distance of social conditions and the duration of political action are long-winded: in short, the wherewithal to discourage for ever any idea of subversion.

I see nothing in any of this which distances it from the basic aspirations of the theoretician of monarchy and despotism. The 'regime of the future'[16] is, indeed, in many ways different from the monarchies of the Europe of the time. The latter still have the feel of their origins and their rudimentary constitutions are still primitive: they are poorly armed to fight the danger of despotism which threatens them and to resolve the complex problems of the modern world. But they can be said to contain in them, in their political and social structure, everything needed to satisfy this exigency. The representation of the *people* itself which seems to contradict all his past positions, and has led some people to believe that Montesquieu was a republican at heart and on the side of the third estate, is in the spirit of monarchy. Read Chapter 8 of Book XI, whose sixth chapter was precisely the one with the discussion of the English Constitution, and it will be clear that the principle of the *representatives* of a nation in a monarchy, a principle entirely foreign to antiquity, belongs to the very origins of *Gothic* government, 'the best species of constitution that could possibly be imagined by man' (SL, XI, 8). That is why Montesquieu can say of the government which seems to look forward to the future, that the English found it 'in the woods' of their past (SL, XI, 6).

16. Prélot, op. cit., p. 123.

Thus the analysis of the English Constitution leads essentially to the same point as the examination of monarchy and despotism; to the same point as certain of the reasons behind the theoretical principles of the opponent of the theorists of the social contract: *to Montesquieu's political choice.*

This political choice may be masked for two reasons. First, Montesquieu's mode of reflection, the juridical purity and abstraction of his political analyses. I think that my more careful examination has shown that Montesquieu's juridicalism itself in its own way expresses his *parti pris*. But this choice may also be concealed by history: by the history that separates us from Montesquieu; and the history that Montesquieu himself lived. To understand this choice properly, it must be grasped in itself and in the history Montesquieu lived: in the history which he thought he was living, whereas it too was also acting on him behind his back.

Chapter Six

Montesquieu's *Parti Pris*

We have now certainly made some progress. From the separation of powers to the equilibrium of the *puissances* dividing up the power. And from this apparent equilibrium to the scheme to re-establish and consecrate one among these *puissances*: the nobility. But we are still within Montesquieu.

In this examination we have managed to move from the fore-stage to backstage, from our author's apparent reasons to his real reasons. But in doing so we have adopted his reasons and accepted the division of roles he proposed for us without adapting them in any way. Take Eisenmann, for example: he has a notion that the problem is not juridical, but political and social. But when it comes to listing the social forces present he rediscovers Montesquieu's own three forces: king, nobility, bourgeoisie, and goes no further. Moreover, this tripartition is not Montesquieu's alone, it is the tripartition of the whole epoch, of Voltaire, Helvétius, Diderot and Condorcet, and of a long tradition lasting well into the nineteenth century and perhaps still not quite dead even today. This conviction is so manifest, this obviousness so general, that none of the parties in the eighteenth century, even up to the beginning of the Revolution, ever thought of revoking it. Should we therefore accept it absolutely? Can we go so straightforwardly into the categories of Montesquieu and his age and decide without argument that he very accurately *distinguished the puissances*, not in their combination, but in their *definition*, and separated them according to their 'natural articulations'?

What I mean is that we should pose ourselves a very simple question, but one which may turn everything upside down: *do the categories in which the men of the eighteenth century thought the history they were living answer to the historical reality?* In particular is the clear distinction between the three *puissances* a well-founded one? Is the king really a *puissance* in the same sense as the nobility and the bourgeoisie? Is the king an autonomous *puissance* of his own, sufficiently distinct from the others not in person or powers, but in *role and function*, that he can really be put in the balance with the others, be circumvented and compacted with? The 'bourgeoisie' itself, those notables of profession (*la robe*), trade and finance, is it to that extent and *in that epoch* the opponent of the nobility and its opposite already detectable in the lower chamber Montesquieu concedes it, its first theoretical victory in a campaign which was to triumph in the Revolution? To ask these questions is to call back into doubt the very convictions of the men of the eighteenth century and to raise the difficult problem of the nature of *absolute monarchy* on the one hand, of the *bourgeoisie* on the other, in the historical period in which Montesquieu lived and which he thinks.

Now we have to admit that one *idea* dominated all the political literature of the eighteenth century: the idea that absolute monarchy was set up *against the nobility*, and that the king relied on the *commoners* to balance the power of his feudal opponents and reduce them to his mercy. The great dispute between the *Romanists* and the *Germanists* about the origins of feudalism and absolute monarchy unfolded against the background of this general conviction. Its echo can be found in many passages in the *Spirit of Laws*;[1] and in its last three Books, which are hardly ever read but are devoted entirely to it, and should be read to see on which side Montesquieu really ranged himself. On the one hand the *Germanists* (Saint-Simon, Boulainvilliers and Montesquieu, the last better informed and more nuanced, but just as firm) nostalgically evoke the age of *primitive* monarchy: a king elected by the nobles and a peer among his peers, as it was originally in the 'forests' of Germany, counterposing it to monarchy become

---

1. SL, VI, 18; X, 3; XI, 7 & 9; XIV, 14; XVII, 5; XVIII, 22; etc.

absolute: a king fighting with and sacrificing the great to take his clerks and his allies from the commoners.[2] On the other hand the absolutist party, *bourgeois* in inspiration, the *Romanists* (the Abbé Dubos, that author of a 'conspiracy . . . against the nobility' – SL, XXX, 10 – and target of the last Books of the *Spirit of Laws*), and the Encyclopedists, celebrate either in Louis XIV or in the *enlightened despot* the ideal of a prince who is wise enough to prefer the merits and titles of the hard-working *bourgeoisie* to the outdated pretensions of the feudal lords. These *partis pris* are incompatible, but the argument is the same. But we are justified in asking whether this basic conflict opposing the king to the nobility and this supposed alliance between absolute monarchy and the bourgeoisie against the feudal lords *does not mask the true relation of forces.*

We should not conceal from ourselves the fact that contemporaries of the time *lived* their history while *thinking* it, and that their thought, still groping for scientific criteria, lacked that necessary distance which enables thought to become the *critique* of life. Thinking a history whose deeper springs escaped them, it was easy for them to limit their thought *to the immediate categories* of their historical life, most often taking political intentions for reality itself, and superficial conflicts for the basis of things. History and the perceived world are not so very different. Everyone can immediately and obviously 'see' in history 'forms', 'structures', groups of men, tendencies and conflicts. It is to this obviousness that Montesquieu appeals in his famous statement: 'There are three species of government; . . . in order to discover their nature, it is sufficient to recollect the idea of them had by the least educated of men' (SL, 11, 1). It is this kind of obviousness which makes visible the omnipotence of a king, nobles slaves to a court or reduced to a minimal political portion on their lands, omnipotent and mischievous intendants, upstart commoners. It is enough to have one's eyes open to see these *facts*, as it is enough

2. Cf. SL, XXXI, 21: Louis the Debonnaire, 'As he had no longer any confidence in the nobility, he promoted mean people, turning the nobles out of their employments at court to make room for strangers and upstarts.'

to have one's eyes open to the world to perceive immediately forms, objects, groups and movements: this obviousness, which does without knowledge, can nonetheless lay claim to it and think that it *understands* what it only *perceives*. But the elements at least of a *science* are really needed to understand the deeper nature of these obviousnesses, to distinguish between the profound structures and conflicts on the one hand and the superficial ones on the other, and between the real motions and the apparent motions. Without a *critique* of the immediate concepts in which every epoch thinks the history it lives, we shall remain on the threshold of a true knowledge of history and a prisoner of the illusions it produces in the men who live it.

I believe that in order to cast light on the ideological problems of this period, it is helpful precisely to draw on the recent achievements of historical research, and to re-examine the received notions of absolute monarchy, of its 'alliance with the bourgeoisie' and of the nature of that bourgeoisie itself.

I must content myself with very brief indications. However, I do want to say that it seems more or less certain today that the gravest danger confronting the historian of the seventeeth and even of the eighteenth century, at least of its first half, is to project onto the 'bourgeoisie' of this period the image of the later bourgeoisie which made the Revolution, and of the bourgeoisie which emerged from the Revolution. The true modern bourgeoisie, which transformed the previous economic and social order from top to bottom, is the *industrial* bourgeoisie, with its mass-production economy, concentrating entirely on profit subsequently reinvested in production. But in its generality this bourgeoisie was unknown to the eighteenth century; the bourgeoisie of that period was quite different: in its most advanced elements it was essentially dependent on the *mercantile economy*. The fact that the industrial economy emerged at a given moment from an accumulation in which the mercantile economy constituted a moment, too often gives rise to the conclusion that the mercantile economy was foreign to feudal society in principle. Nothing is more doubtful. Once we know in what sense this mercantile economy then acted we see that it was a fairly well intergrated part of the feudal system itself: mercantilism is precisely the politics and theory of this integration. All the economic activity which then seemed to constitute the vanguard (commerce, manufactures) was indeed concentrated on the State apparatus, subordinate to its profits and to its needs.[3] Manufactures were founded above all to provide the court with luxury goods, the troops with arms and the royal commerce with materials for exports, the profits from which returned to the treasury. The great navigation companies were created first and foremost to bring into the country, and always more or less to the advantage of the royal administration, spices and precious metals from overseas. *In its structure the economic cycle of this period is thus orientated towards the State apparatus as its goal.* And the counterpart to this orientation is the fact that the 'bourgeois' who at one moment or another give life to these economic operations have *no other economic or individual horizon than the feudal order that this State apparatus serves:* on becoming rich, the merchant does not, *with a few rare exceptions,* invest his gains in private production, but *in lands,* which he buys for their title and for an entry into the nobility; *in offices* that are functions of the administration, which he buys so as to enjoy their revenue as a kind of rent; and *in State loans,* which guarantee him large profits. The aim of the 'bourgeois' enriched by trade thus consists of *directly entering the society of the nobility,* by the purchase of lands or the refurbishing of a family whose daughter he marries, or of *directly entering the State apparatus* by the gown and offices, or of *sharing in the profits of the State apparatus* via rents. This is what gives this upstart 'bourgeoisie' such a peculiar situation in the feudal State: it takes its place inside the nobility more than it fights it, and with these pretensions to enter the order it seems to be fighting, it supports it as much as it undermines it: the whole cycle of its economic activity and of the careers of its members

3. 'The laws' in a monarchy 'ought to favour all kinds of commerce consistent with the constitution, to the end that the subjects may, without ruining themselves, be able to satisfy the continual cravings of the prince and his court' (SL, V, 9).

thus remains inscribed *in the limits and structures of the feudal State*.

Once established, this point obviously overthrows both the classical schema of the alliance between the absolute monarchy and the bourgeoisie, and the received notion of *absolute monarchy*. It is therefore necessary to ask what is the nature and function of *absolute monarchy*, even in the conflicts which at this time oppose it to the nobility.

Up to the present, two answers have been given to this question. Both abandon the idea of the king, in the grotesque caricature of the despot, as the sworn enemy of the feudal lords, replacing it by the idea that the fundamental conflict of this period did not oppose the king to the feudal lords, but the feudal lords to the rising 'bourgeoisie', to the people. But the agreement goes no further.

For the first interpretation sees in this conflict the origin and opportunity of absolute monarchy. The confrontation and involuntary equilibrium of two antagonistic classes, each powerless to triumph over the other, and the peril in which their struggle put the entire society, gave the king the opportunity to raise himself above them as the arbiter in their rivalry, and to draw all his strength from each of their powers opposed or threatened by the power of the other.[4] It is this exceptional situation which explains how the king could play one class off against the other and sustain the hopes of each at the very moment he was playing the other's game. This explains why *all parties in the eighteenth century* fought over the king, both those who wanted to see him turn back towards the origin of his institutions, and restore the nobility to its rights, and those who expected his *enlightenment* would give the victory to bourgeois reason against privilege and arbitrariness. The fund of ideas common to both right-wing

4. See even in Marx (*The German Ideology*, London, 1965, pp. 60–1) a passage on Montesquieu which still (in 1845) inclines towards this interpretation: 'For instance, in an age and in a country where royal power, aristocracy and bourgeoisie are contending for mastery and where, therefore, mastery is shared, the doctrine of the separation of powers proves to be the dominant idea and is expressed as an "eternal law".'

(feudal) and left-wing (bourgeois) combatants related not to dominant and shared illusions, but to the reality of an absolute monarch who, thanks to an irresoluble balance of forces, has become the real arbiter between the two opposed classes. But this interpretation has the weakness that it lapses into an idea of the bourgeoisie which, as I believe I have indicated, does not correspond to the reality.

Much more illuminating is the second answer, which has acquired additional authority from Porshnev's recent studies on the *Fronde* and *Popular Revolts in France in the seventeenth and eighteenth centuries.*[5] In this view, the thesis of the king as arbiter between two equally strong and equally powerless opposed classes is based both on an anachronism and on a mythical notion of the nature of the State. The anachronism, as I have shown, is to lend the *bourgeoisie* of absolute monarchy the traits of the later bourgeoisie, *in order to think it even in this epoch as a class radically antagonistic to the feudal class*. We know all about this. The mythical notion of the nature of the State is to imagine that a political power can be established and exercised outside classes and over them, even in the general interests of society. This dual critique leads to the following perspective: absolute monarchy is not the end, nor is its aim the end, of the regime of feudal exploitation. On the contrary, in the period under consideration it is its *indispensable political apparatus*. What changes with the appearance of absolute monarchy is not the regime of feudal exploitation, it is *the form of its political domination*. The primitive monarchy celebrated by the *Germanists*, the personal political privileges of feudal lords enjoying an independence that made them the king's *peers*, has merely given way to a centralized, dominant and absolute monarchy. This political transformation was a response to changes in the conditions of economic activity which occurred inside the feudal regime itself, and in particular to the development of the mercantile economy, the first appearance of a national market, etc. In the period under consideration, these modifications do not make any inroads into feudal exploitation

5. See bibliography.

itself. And the political regime of absolute monarchy is merely the new political form required to maintain feudal domination and exploitation in a period of the development of the mercantile economy.

It is hardly surprising that the advent of absolute monarchy, centralization and its epiphenomena (and even that gilded political internment camp, Versailles) had the appearances of a usurpation, an injustice and a violence directed at their class in the eyes of the individual feudal lords, stripped, even by force, of their ancient personal political prerogatives. But it is impossible not to reckon this precisely *a fixed idea of theirs which masked the real from them, and a true historical misunderstanding which made them confuse these ancient personal political prerogatives with the general interests of their class.* For it is only too clear that the king of absolute monarchy represented the *general interests of the feudal class* up to and including against the protestations of the individual feudal lords with their old-fashioned nostalgia and blindness. And if the king was an *arbiter*, he was not the arbiter in the conflict between the nobility and the bourgeoisie, but in *conflicts within the feudal class*, which he resolved in its interest. When he decided, it was, in general, never for anything but to guarantee the future of that class and of its domination, even against some of its members.

But here another *puissance* intervenes, one which Montesquieu does not introduce into the division of power, another *puissance* than those that won the honours of political theory: the '*puissance*' of the masses of the people who were precisely the victims of the feudal exploitation which it was the function of the State apparatus and absolute monarchy to maintain and perpetuate. Porshnev has partly restated and partly discovered this aspect of the problem, showing that *the fundamental antagonism at that time did not counterpose the absolute monarchy to the feudal lords, nor the nobility to a bourgeoisie which was for the most part integrated into the regime of feudal exploitation and profited by it, but the feudal regime itself to the masses subject to its exploitation.* This fundamental conflict does not stand out like the secondary conflicts, nor does it have their theoreticians. And it does not take the same forms. Between the king, the nobility and the *bourgeoisie* all was decided by a constant conflict of a *political* and *ideological* kind. Between the masses of the exploited, peasants subject to feudal rights, small craftsmen, shopkeepers, minor professions in the towns, on the one hand, and the feudal order and its political power on the other, it was hardly a question of theoretical disputes but rather a matter of silence or violence. It was a struggle between power and poverty, most often settled by submission and for brief periods by riots and arms. Now these starvation rebellions were very frequent in town and country throughout the seventeenth century in France, which had not only the peasants' wars and jacqueries of sixteenth-century Germany, but also urban riots; these risings were ruthlessly suppressed. Now we can see what the king, the *absolute* power, and the *State apparatus* were for, and what side the famous *'puissances'* which occupied the forestage were on; until certain *'journées révolutionnaires'* of the Revolution, the first that achieved a victory – and brought a certain disorder both to theories and powers.

The privilege of this fourth *'puissance'*, which so concerned the thoughts of the other three, was to be, so to speak, not represented in the political literature of the period. Not until the appearance of a poor priest from Champagne, like Meslier, whose Testament Voltaire carefully purged of all its political sting, and then Rousseau, did this 'people', this 'common people' (*bas-peuple*) enter as a *puissance*, first into pamphlets, and finally into the concepts of political theory. Before this it had only an allusive existence theoretically: as it does in Montesquieu himself, who is so careful strictly to distinguish the notables from it. As it does for Voltaire and most of the Encyclopedists. But this fourth *puissance*, this subject of non-knowledge, passion and violence, nevertheless haunts the alliances of the other three as a memory does its loss: by its censorship. The reason why this *puissance* is absent from the contracts that concern it is that the reason for these contracts was to make it absent – or, what is the same thing, to consecrate its slavery.

It seems to me that if we bear in mind this *real* nature of the forces invoked by Montesquieu: the king, the nobility, the 'bourgeoisie' and the 'common people', some light will be cast on our general interpretation of his political choice and influence.

This real analysis enables us to evade the appearances of retrospective history. And in particular the illusion of believing Montesquieu to be *the herald, even the disguised herald, of the cause of the bourgeoisie which was to triumph under the Revolution.* It is clear what the famous lower chamber, already so well framed in the project of an English-style constitution,[6] represents: the share offered to a bourgeoisie which was seeking its place in the feudal order and, finding it there, hardly dreamt of threatening that order any further. This perspective also enables us to judge at their real historical value the liberal 'reforms' for which Montesquieu set himself up as spokesman: the reform of penal legislation, the critique of war, etc. They were so little related to the future triumphs of the bourgeoisie that the very same Montesquieu who reckoned torture inhuman intended that the nobles should have their own class tribunal in every matter: the upper chamber. What has made it look as if Montesquieu belonged to the party of the 'bourgeoisie' seems to me rather to have been conceived by him partly as common-sense proposals in which he had the public courage of his convictions, partly as a rather skilful way precisely of bringing the 'bourgeoisie' round to his cause and swelling the feudal opposition with the contribution of the discontents of this 'bourgeoisie'. Which presupposes, if not a clear vision, at least a fairly real sense of the objectives of this bourgeoisie.

But this analysis also enables us to understand the paradox of

6. 'England is at present the freest country there is in the world . . . but if the lower house gains the upper hand, its power would be unlimited and dangerous; instead, at present unlimited power is invested in the King and parliament, and the executive power (*puissance*) in the King, whose power is limited' (Notes on England, Pléiade edition, op. cit., vol. 1, p. 884). Cf. also the instructive example of primitive monarchies: 'The people there were the legislative *puissance*' (SL, XI, 11). But 'as soon as the people got the legislative power into their hands, they might, as they everywhere did, upon the very least caprice, subvert the regal authority' (ibid.). That is because, in these monarchies of heroic Greece, there was not yet any 'body of nobles' (SL, XI, 8). The representation of the people, even by notables, was thus not balanced within the legislature by the representation of the nobility.

Montesquieu's posterity. For this right-wing opponent served all the left-wing opponents for the rest of the century, before providing weapons in future history for all reactionaries. Of course, in the most acute period of the Revolution, Montesquieu disappeared. Robespierre speaks very harshly of the division of powers: we can hear the disciple of Rousseau confronting a situation in which theories could be judged. But it remains the case that the whole pre-revolutionary period was acted out very largely *in terms of Montesquieu's themes*, and this feudal enemy of despotism became the hero of all the opponents of the established order. By a unique historical *volte-face*, a man who looked towards the past seemed to open the door to the future. I believe that this paradox pertains above all to ·the *anachronistic* character of Montesquieu's position. It is because he pleaded the cause of *an outdated order* that he set himself up as an opponent of a political order *which others were to make outdated*. With due allowance, his thought is like the revolt of the nobility which preceded the Revolution, and which Mathiez argues precipitated it. Montesquieu himself merely wanted to re-establish a threatened nobility in its outdated rights. But he thought the threat came from the king. In fact, taking sides against the king's absolute power, he lent his hand to the undermining of the State apparatus which was the nobility's only rampart. His contemporaries made no mistake about this when, like Helvétius, they reckoned him 'too feudal',[7] and yet they conscripted him in their battles. What does it matter where the blows come from so long as they strike the same point? And if it is true that this 'revolutionary' posterity of Montesquieu's is a misunderstanding, that misunderstanding must nonetheless be given its due: it was merely the *truth* of an earlier misunderstanding: the misunderstanding that had projected Montesquieu into right-wing opposition at a time when it no longer had any meaning.

7. *Réflexions Morales*, CXLVII. Cf. also his letters to Montesquieu and Saurin.

Conclusion

And if I should close by returning to my first words, let me say of this man who set out alone and truly discovered the new lands of history, that nevertheless his own notion was always to return home. The conquered land he salutes on his last page, as I pretended to forget, was the land of return. Such a long route to come back home. To old-fashioned ideas after so many new ideas. To the past after so much future. As if this traveller, having set out for distant lands, and spent many years in the unknown, believed on returning home that time had stood still.

But he had broken the trail.

Bibliography

WORKS BY MONTESQUIEU IN FRENCH AND ENGLISH

Oeuvres Complètes, 2 vols, ed. Roger Caillois, Pléiade edn, Paris, 1949–51.

De l'esprit des lois, ed. G. Truc, Classiques Garnier, Paris, 1964.

The Spirit of Laws, translated by Thomas Nugent, revised by J. V. Pritchard, Encyclopaedia Britannica, Chicago, 1952.

Lettres Persanes, ed. Jacques Roger, Garnier-Flammarion, Paris, 1964.

Persian Letters, translated by C. J. Betts, Penguin Classics, Harmondsworth, 1973.

Considérations sur les Causes de la Grandeur des Romains et de leur Décadence, ed. Ehrard, Garnier-Flammarion, Paris, 1969.

Considerations on the Causes of the Greatness of the Romans and their Decline, translated with notes and introduction by David Lowenthal, Collier-Macmillan, New York and London, 1965.

WORKS ON MONTESQUIEU

Individual Authors

Henri Barckhausen, *Montesquieu: ses idées at ses œuvres d'après les papiers de La Brède* (Paris, 1907).

Pierre François Barrière, *Un Grand provincial: Charles-Louis de Secondat, baron de la Brède at de Montesquieu* (Bordeaux, 1946).

Ély Carcassonne, *Montesquieu et le problème de la Constitution française au XVIIIe siècle* (Paris, 1927).

Ernst Cassirer, *The Philosophy of the Enlightenment*, translated by Fritz C. A. Koelln and James P. Pettegrove (Princeton N.J., 1951).

Sergio Cotta, *Montesquieu e la scienza della società* (Turin, 1953).

Joseph Dedieu, *Montesquieu et la tradition politique anglaise en France. Les sources anglaises de l'Esprit des Lois* (Paris, 1909).

Dino Del Bo, *Montesquieu, le dottrine politiche e giuridiche* (Milan, 1943).

Émile Durkheim, *Montesquieu and Rousseau, Forerunners of Sociology*, translated by R. Manheim (Ann Arbor, 1960).

Charles Eisenmann, 'L'Esprit des Lois et la séparation des pouvoirs,' *Mélanges R. Carré de Malberg* (Paris, 1933), pp. 163–92.

Bernhard Groethuysen, *Montesquieu*, Introduction to a selection of texts in the collection 'Les classiques de la liberté' (Geneva, 1947).

Paul Hazard, *European Thought in the Eighteenth Century*, translated by J. Lewis May (Harmondsworth 1965).

Maxime Leroy, *Histoire des idées sociales en France: I. De Montesquieu à Robespierre* (Paris, 1946).

Boris Fedorovich Porshnev, *Jean Meslier et les sources populaires de ses idées* (Address to the Rome Congress, 1955; French edition by the Academy of the Sciences of the USSR).

Boris Fedorovich Porshnev, *Les soulèvements populaires en France de 1623 à 1648*, translated by Ranieta, revised Robert Mandrou, École Pratique des Hautes Études, Centre de Recherches Historiques Oeuvres étrangères, no. 4 (Paris 1963). On Porshnev, see *La Pensée* nos. 32, 40 & 41.

Charles Seignobos, 'La séparation des pouvoirs,' in *Études de politique et d'histoire*, ed. J. Letaconnoux (Paris, 1934).

Jean Starobinski, *Montesquieu par lui-même* (Paris, 1953).

Charles Edward Vaughan, *Studies in the History of Political Philosophy before and after Rousseau*, ed. Λ. G. Little (Manchester, 1925), vol. 1.

Enrico Vidal, *Saggio sul Montesquieu, con particolare riguardo alla sua concezione dell'uomo, del diritto e della politica* (Milan, 1950).

Collective Works

Revue de métaphysique et de morale, special number of October 1939 on Montesquieu.

'Montesquieu: sa pensée politique et constitutionnelle,' *Recueil Sirey du bi-centenaire de l'Esprit des Lois* (Paris, 1952).

Bulletin de droit tchécoslovaque, Bicentenary of Montesquieu's Death, in French (Prague, 1955).

Actes du Congrès Montesquieu (Bordeaux, 1956).

Part Two

Rousseau: The Social Contract
(The Discrepancies)

Foreword

In interrogating the philosophy we have inherited, we can start from one simple observation: each great doctrine itself thinks itself in a specifically *philosophical* object and in its theoretical effects. For example: the Platonic Idea, Aristotelean Action, the Cartesian Cogito, the Kantian Transcendental Subject, etc. These objects have no theoretical existence outside the domain of philosophy proper. Within Rousseau's doctrine, the *Social Contract* is a theoretical object of the same kind: elaborated and constructed by a philosophical reflection which draws from it certain definite theoretical effects.[1]

I should like to suggest *vis-à-vis* Rousseau's philosophical object, the 'Social Contract', that an examination of the mode of theoretical functioning of the fundamental philosophical object of a theory may enlighten us as to the objective function of that philosophical theory: to be quite precise, as to the problems it eludes in the very 'problems' it elects.

Indeed, a schematic analysis of the theoretical functioning of the object *Social Contract* confronts us with the following fact: this functioning is only possible because of the 'play' of an internal theoretical discrepancy (Discrepancy I).[2] The 'solution'

1. The material which has gone into the following pages is taken from a course of lectures given at the École Normale Supérieure, Paris, in 1965–6.
2. *Translator's note: Décalage.* In *Reading Capital* and *Lenin and Philosophy and Other Essays*, I translated this word as 'dislocation'. Its literal meaning is something like the state of being 'staggered' or 'out of step'. I have shifted from a more mechanical to a more mental metaphor in my translation here because it makes the sense of the term in this essay emerge much more clearly, but also because the standard English translations of Lenin use 'discrepancy' to translate the Russian *nesootvetstvie*, where Lenin is clearly using the word for the concept embodied by all Althusser's

of the political 'problem' by the 'social contract' is only possible because of the theoretical 'play' of this Discrepancy. However, the 'Social Contract' has the immediate function of masking the play of the Discrepancy which alone enables it to function. To mask means to denegate and reject. In fact, the functioning of the Social Contract in Discrepancy I is only possible because this Discrepancy I is carried over and transposed in the form of a Discrepancy II, which alone enables the corresponding solution to function theoretically. Discrepancy II then leads by the same mechanism to a Discrepancy III, which, on the same principle still, leads to a Discrepancy IV. We thus find that we are confronted by the observation of a chain of theoretical discrepancies, each new discrepancy being charged to make the corresponding solution, itself an effect of an earlier solution, 'function'. In the chain of 'solutions' (Social Contract, alienation-exchange, general will-particular will, etc.) we thus discern the presence of another chain, one which makes the first theoretically possible: the chain of pertinent Discrepancies which at each stage enable the corresponding solutions to 'function' theoretically. A comparison of these two chains, of the 'logic' peculiar to each, and of the very special logic of their relationship (the theoretical repression of the Discrepancy) direct us towards an understanding of the theoretical function of the philosophical system in which Rousseau proposed to think politics.

If this type of analysis proved well-founded, it would also have the following dual interest:

1. It would make intelligible Rousseau's problematic and the

uses of '*décalage*', e. g.: 'We, the Russian proletariat, are in *advance* of any Britain or any Germany as regards our political order, as regards the strength of the workers' political power, but we are *behind* the most backward West-European country in organizing a good state capitalism, as regards our level of culture and the degree of material and productive preparedness for the "introduction" of socialism. . . . It would be a fatal mistake to declare that since there is a *discrepancy* between our economic "forces" and our political forces, it "follows" that we should not have seized power. Such an argument can be advanced only by "a man in a muffler" who forgets that there will always be such a "discrepancy", and that it always exists in the development of nature as well as in the developments of society' (' "Left-wing" Childishness and Petty-Bourgeois Mentality', in *Collected Works*, vol. 27, London 1965, pp. 346–7).

theoretical effects of that problematic (including the apparently technical arrangements for the organization of power, the distinction between its organs, its working procedures).

2. It would make intelligible the possibility of a number of 'readings' of Rousseau's *Social Contract*, and the subsequent interpretations (Kantian, Hegelian, etc.). These interpretations will no longer seem to us to be merely arbitrary or tendentious, but as founded in their possibility in Rousseau's text itself: to be quite precise, in the 'play' allowed by the 'space' of the theoretical Discrepancies constitutive of Rousseau's theory. In their turn, the interpretations may provide us with an index and proof of the necessary existence of those Discrepancies.

My analysis will essentially concern Book I, Chapter VI of the *Social Contract*.

Chapter One

Posing the Problem

A. RESULT OF CHAPTERS I–V

Book I Chapter IV sustains the whole of the *Social Contract*, since it poses and resolves the problem which constitutes the fundamental question (that 'theoretical abyss') of political life.

This fundamental question is posed in the following terms:

The problem is to find a form of association which will defend and protect with the whole common force the person and goods of each associate, and in which each, while uniting himself with all, may still obey himself alone, and remain as free as before. This is the fundamental problem of which the Social Contract provides the solution (SC I, VI, p. 90).[1]

But Chapter VI, which formulates the question in this way, has five chapters preceding it.

Chapter I only promises the solution:

. . . the social order is a sacred right which is the basis of all other rights. Nevertheless, this right does not come from nature, and must therefore be founded on conventions. Before coming to that, I have to prove what I have just asserted (SC I, I, pp. 3–4).

Rousseau proves it in Chapters II–V: a refusal to found society in nature, or in illegitimate conventions.

In Chapter II, Rousseau shows that society cannot have the family as its origin. In Chapter III, that it cannot be founded on the 'right of the strongest'. In Chapter IV, that it cannot depend on 'conventions' sanctioning the effects of violence (the submission of the slave to his master, of a nation to its conqueror).

In Chapter V, Rousseau draws the conclusion: 'That we must

---

1. Page references are to Jean-Jacques Rousseau, *The Social Contract and Discourses*, translated by G. D. H. Cole, London, 1966.

always go back to a first convention', first in principle with respect to all possible conventions, in particular with respect to that convention called the 'contract of subjugation' which, according to Grotius, a people might conclude with the king to whom it submits.

It would be better, before examining the act by which a people gives itself to a king, to examine that by which a people is a people; for this act, being necessarily prior to the other, is the true foundation of society (SC I, V, p. 11).

And, in the final paragraph of this same Chapter V, Rousseau rejects one last objection concerning the majority principle:

The law of majority voting is itself something established by convention, and presupposes unanimity, on one occasion at least (SC I, V, p. 11).

With this last thesis Rousseau is rejecting the Lockean theory of the 'natural' character ('natural' in the physical sense of the word) of the law of the majority. The majority does not belong to the social body as weight does to the physical body. It presupposes an act of convention prior in principle to its stipulation: it therefore presupposes a unanimous act of convention which adopts it as a law.

Having set aside every hypothetical natural foundation for the social body and rejected the classical recourse to false contracts derived from force, Chapter V thus leads to two results:

1. It is necessary to elucidate the question of the primordial contract, prior in principle to every contract: the contract concluded in *'the act by which a people is a people'*.

2. Since the law of the majority can only act on the basis of a first unanimous convention which adopts and establishes it, the contract by which 'a people is a people' implies *unanimity*.

B. POSING THE PROBLEM

Chapter VI can then pose the problem in all its rigour. This posing contains three moments: (a) the conditions for posing the problem; (b) the absolute limits to posing the problem; and (c) the posing of the problem properly speaking.

(a) *The conditions for posing the problem*

They are expressed in the first paragraph of Chapter VI.

I suppose men to have reached the point at which the obstacles in the way of their preservation in the state of nature show their power of resistance to be greater than the forces at the disposal of each individual for his maintenance in that state. That primitive condition can then subsist no longer; and the human race would perish unless it changed its manner of existence (SC I, VI, p. 11).

Let us examine the important terms in these two sentences, which define the objective conditions for posing the problem.

The first condition is that 'men' have 'reached' a 'point' which is nothing but a limit-point, a critical point in their existence: the point dividing the life of the human race from its death. This fatal critical 'point' for the human race takes us back to the *Discourse on Inequality*: it is the fully developed *state of war*.

This point is critical and fatal because it is the site of an insurmountable contradiction in that state between on the one hand the 'obstacles' in the way of the life of the human race, and on the other the 'forces' that individuals can oppose to them. What are these *'obstacles'*? What are these *'forces'*?

(i) *The 'obstacles'*

They are not external obstacles. They do not come from nature (catastrophes, cataclysms, 'natural' difficulties – climate, resources – in the production of sustenance, etc.). We know that Nature has been tamed, she is no longer at war with herself, once men have cultivated her: the only catastrophes left are human ones. Nor do the 'obstacles' come from other human groups.

They are purely internal to existing human relations. They have a name: they are the effects of the generalized state of war, of universal competition and, even in the breathing-space of a precarious 'peace', the constant threat which everyone feels hanging over his goods, his liberty and his life. State of war must be understood in the strong sense, as Hobbes was the first to define it: this state is a constant and universal relation existing between men, i.e. it is independent of individuals, even if they are peaceful. This state defines their very condition: they are subject and condemned to it, unable either to find any shelter in the world to protect them from its implacable effects or to hope for any respite from the evils afflicting them.

These 'obstacles' stand 'in the way of' the 'preservation' of men 'in the state of nature'. What the state of war threatens is what constitutes the ultimate essence of man: his free life, his life as such, the instinct that 'preserves' him alive, what Rousseau calls 'self-respect' (*amour de soi*) in the *Discourse on Inequality*.

I shall take the liberty of calling this state of perpetual and universal war the state of human *alienation*. This is a theoretical 'anticipation'. Although Rousseau does speak and make use of the concept of alienation, he does not do so to designate the effects of that state of war. I shall give reasons for the liberty I am thus taking.

(ii) *The 'forces'*

These 'resistant' 'obstacles' are opposed by the 'forces' at the disposal of 'each individual' for his maintenance in the state of nature.

These forces are constituted by the attributes of the natural man, having arrived at the state of war. Without this last specification, the problem of the Social Contract is incomprehensible.

When, in the *Social Contract*, Rousseau mentions these 'forces' it is clear that he is not mentioning the 'forces' of man in the 'first state of nature' in which we find no more than a free animal, with zero 'intellectual and moral faculties'. We are concerned with an animal which the double impact of the Natural Catastrophes and the Great Discovery (metallurgy) has made a social being with developed and alienated faculties. The animal of the first state of nature has as its 'forces': its body (life) + its liberty. The man of the generalized state of war has quite different forces. He still has his body (though his physical powers have declined), but he has intellectual forces and also *'goods'*, too. 'Each member of the community gives himself to it, at the moment of its foundation, just as he is, with all the forces at his command, including the goods he possesses' (SC I, IX, p. 16). He has 'acquired' these goods during the development of his social existence, which induced the development of his intellectual and 'moral' faculties.

The 'forces' of the individual in the state of war can thus be resumed as follows: physical forces (life) + intellectual and 'moral' forces + goods + liberty. Liberty still features alongside 'force': 'The force and liberty of each man are the chief instruments of his self-preservation' (SC I, VI, p. 12).

I have not made this comparison for the fun of noting distinctions, but because their registration is the index of a development —the *alienation* of man even within the state of nature, as a result of the historical process which culminates in the state of war.

We can grasp this transformation in the presence of 'goods' among the 'forces' of the individual, and in the appearance of a new category of human existence: the category of *interest*. 'If the opposition of particular interests made the establishments of societies necessary . . . ' (SC II, I, p. 20). It is enough to put this definition of the condition of the Contract (the opposition of particular interests) alongside the effects of the generalized state of war to see that while the process of the socialization of men transformed their faculties, it simultaneously transformed their 'self-respect' into particular interest. When particular interest is reflected by the individual, it takes the abstract (and subjective) form of egoism (*amour propre*), the alienation of self-respect (*amour de soi*). But the objective content of particular interest links it directly with the nature of the state of war. The category of particular interest immediately betrays its universal basis. One particular interest can only exist as a function of the other particular interests in rivalry, in universal competition. This is revealed by the sentence of Rousseau's I have just quoted: 'The opposition of particular interests . . . ' means that particular interest is constituted by the universal opposition which is the essence of the state of war. There are not first individuals each with his own particular interest: opposition intervening subsequently as an accident. The opposition is primary: it is the opposition that constitutes the individual as a particular individual with a particular interest. Remembering the exclusive seizure of lands (taken away from the 'supernumeraries') which induces the state of war in the universal sense of a state, and all its subsequent effects: rich and poor, strong and weak, masters and slaves, it is clear what meaning is concealed by the apparently anodyne inclusion of 'goods' in the list of the elements constituting the 'forces' of the individuals when they have reached the state of war.

It is important to mark the category of particular interest as specific to the state of social ties existing in the state of war. Literally speaking, the human animal of the first state of nature has no particular *interest* because nothing can oppose him to other men – the condition of all opposition, i.e. of necessary ties, being then still absent. Only developed-alienated man acquires little by little, as a result of the ties in which he is engaged by the dialectic of involuntary socialization, the advantage (if such it can be called) of the category of particular interest, the form taken by egoism in nascent society. Particular interest only ever truly becomes particular interest in its radicality in the state of war. Particular interest features in so many words in the conditions of the establishment of society: 'If the opposition of particular interests made the establishment of societies necessary, the agreement of these very interests made it possible' (SC II, I, p. 20). Let us bear this text in mind.

(iii) *The fatal contradiction: obstacles/forces*

If the obstacles are purely human and internal, if they are the effects of that state of war, it is clear that the forces of each individual cannot carry him through: for individuals would have to be stronger than the very forces to which they are subject and which make them what they are, each 'stronger' on his own account than the implacable (universal and perpetual) relations in which they are trapped, those of the state of war.

Individuals are trapped in a very special way. These 'obstacles' are not external ones. To specify: there is a close bond between the 'forces' of the individuals and these obstacles, which justifies my speaking of the state of war as a universal state of *alienation*.

What indeed are these universal relations constituting the state of war? These relations in which the individuals are trapped are nothing but the product of their own activities. Hence the relations are not external to the individuals and the individuals cannot change them from the outside. They are co-substantial with the individuals. Indeed, the whole development of human history has been produced by a dialectic such that the effects of the first, involuntary socialization developed but also simultaneously alienated the individual: such that in response this first alienation developed existing social relations while alienating them more and more. So long as 'there was still some forest left', men could partially escape the tyranny of social relations and the alienating effects of their constraint. When the 'end of the forest' came and the whole earth came under cultivation and was seized by its first occupiers or the strong men who supplanted them, then there was no longer any refuge for human liberty. Men were forced into the state of war, i.e. into alienation. That is how they were trapped in the very relations that their activity had produced: they became the *men of those relations, alienated like them*, dominated by their particular interests, powerless against those relations and their effects, exposed at every moment to the fatal contradiction of the state of war. Fatal in the threat it held over their lives and their liberty, henceforth inseparable from the particular interest in which that liberty no longer found anything but its alienated expression. A contradiction in the strict sense of the term, since the state of war is liberty and human activity turned against themselves, threatening and destroying themselves; in the form of their own effects. A contradiction not only between the individuals and their forces on the one hand, and the human 'obstacles' of universal competition on the other, but also (as a function of the nature of this state of universal alienation) between each individual and himself, between self-respect and particular interest, between liberty and death.

Such is the ultimate argument for this critical 'point' at which the 'primitive condition' can 'subsist no longer': 'the human race would perish unless it changed its manner of existence.'

(b) *The absolute limits to posing the problem*

These are the conditions (the state of war on the one hand; the forces of each individual on the other) which define the absolute limits to posing the problem. They are gathered together in the second paragraph of Chapter VI: 'But, as men cannot engender new forces, but only unite and direct existing ones . . . '

What is interesting about this text is that it defines in a rigorous manner the theoretical field of the problem and suggests the impossibility of any solution which introduces an element *external* to that field itself. There is thus no transcendental solution, no recourse to a third party, be it God or Chance. The solution cannot be found outside the existing givens, a ruthless enumeration of which has just been established. The only solution possible inside the theoretical field constituted by men and the alienated relations whose authors and victims they are is for them to change their '*manner of existence*'. Rousseau 'takes men as they are' (SC I, Preface, p. 3). He takes their forces as they are. Men only have these forces at their disposal. No solution in the world can change either the nature of these forces or the nature of the 'obstacles' they collide with. The only way out is to play on the 'manner of existence' of men, or the arrangement of these forces. ' . . . As men cannot engender new forces, but only unite and direct existing ones, they have *no other means* of preserving themselves than the formation, by aggregation, of a sum of forces great enough to overcome the resistance. These they have to bring into play by means of a single motive power, and cause to act in concert' (SC I, VI, pp. 11–12).

The whole of the *Social Contract* is defined by the absolute limits of the theoretical field in which the problem is posed. It is a question of creating a force capable of surmounting the 'obstacles' which block the forces of each individual, of creating this force by inaugurating new relations between the existing forces (union instead of opposition): 'changing the manner of existence' of men. This clearly means posing the problem of the contract as a function of the individuals and of their forces.

(c) *Posing the problem*

What is the existing individual, considered as a subject of definite *forces?* We can summarize the set: life + physical forces + intellectual and moral forces + goods + liberty, in the form: forces + liberty.

And here is the problem definitively posed:

As the force and liberty of each man are the chief instruments of his self-preservation, how can he pledge them without harming his own interests, and neglecting the care he owes to himself? This difficulty, in its bearing on my present subject, may be stated in the following terms:

The problem is to find a form of association which will defend and protect with the whole common force the person and goods of each associate, and in which each, while uniting himself with all, may still obey himself alone, and remain as free as before (SC I, VI, p. 12).

The solution lies in a particular 'form of association' which guarantees the 'unity' of the 'forces' of the individuals without harming the instruments of their self-preservation: their forces (including their goods) and their liberty.

Let us not lose sight of the fact that forces (including goods) + liberty = particular *interest*. Re-read the second sentence of the *Social Contract*: 'In this inquiry I shall endeavour always to unite what right sanctions with what is prescribed by interest, in order that justice and utility may in no case be divided' (p. 3).

Chapter Two

The Solution to the Problem:
Discrepancy I

The solution to the problem posed lies in the nature of the act by which a people is a people: this act is a *contract*.

Apparently Rousseau is here returning to the traditional solution of the school of Natural Law, which thinks the origin of civil society and of the State in the *juridical* concept of the contract.

What does a contract consist of? What are its constitutive elements? Reduced to a schematic expression, a contract is a convention agreed between two Recipient Parties (which I shall call Recipient Party number one or RP 1, and Recipient Party number two or RP 2) in order to proceed to an exchange: give and take. For example, in the classic contract of submission between the People and the Prince, the RP 1 is the People, the RP 2 the Prince. The exchange involves the following 'terms': the People promises obedience to the Prince; the Prince promises to guarantee the good of the People (above all by his respect for the Fundamental Laws). With the sole exception of Hobbes, whose contract has a quite different and quite unprecedented structure, the jurisconsults and philosophers of Natural Law generally respected the juridical structure of the contract (give and take exchange between two RPs) in the use made of the concept of the contract to 'resolve' the problem of the 'origin' of civil and political society.

Rousseau, too, adopts the juridical concept, but immediately warns that 'the clauses of this contract are so determined by the nature of the act that the slightest modification would make them vain and ineffective' (SC I, VI, p. 12). In *Émile* he is more explicit:

'The nature of the social pact is private and peculiar to itself.'[1] In fact, the 'nature of the act' of this contract is such that the structure of the Social Contract in Rousseau is profoundly modified in comparison with its strictly *juridical* model. Behind the juridical concept of the contract we are dealing with an exceptional contract with a paradoxical structure.

The paradox of this peculiar contract lies completely in its central clause.

Its 'clauses, properly understood, may be reduced to one – the *total alienation* of each associate, together with all his rights, to the whole community' (sc I, vI, p. 12).

The mystery of the Social Contract lies in these few words, to be prescise, in the concept of total alienation. This time it is Rousseau himself who speaks of alienation.

What is alienation? Rousseau has already defined the term in Book I Chapter Iv (p. 7):

If an individual, says Grotius, can alienate his liberty and make himself the slave of a master, why could not a whole people do the same and make itself subject to a king? There are in this passage plenty of ambiguous words which would need explaining; but let us confine ourselves to the word *alienate*. To alienate is to give or to sell. Now, a man who becomes the slave of another does not give himself; he sells himself, at least for his sustenance: but for what does a people sell itself?

What emerges from this definition of alienation is the distinction between 'give itself' (as a gratuitous act without exchange) and '*sell itself*' (as a non-gratuitous act, containing the counterpart of an *exchange*). Hence:

To say that a man gives himself gratuitously, is to say what is absurd and inconceivable; such an act is null and illegitimate, from the mere fact that he who does it is out of his mind [or mad. But] madness creates no right (sc I, Iv, p. 7).

Strictly speaking the slave sells himself, since he negotiates his submission at least for his sustenance. Strictly speaking: for

1. Jean-Jacques Rousseau, *Émile*, translated by B. Foxley, London, 1957, p. 425.

this concession of Rousseau's is no more than a demonstrative device, to bring out the fact that even accepting its underlying principle, the thesis of the contract of slavery cannot be extended to the contract of (political) submission. Indeed, a people cannot sell itself: it does not get in exchange for its submission, even from the king, the sustenance that the slave at least receives from his master. A people that thinks it is selling itself (i.e. in an advantageous contract of exchange) is really giving itself for nothing, completely for nothing, including its liberty.

Liberty: it is out, the great word that takes us past the fictions accepted up to this point for the purposes of refuting Grotius. Sell whatever you like (give and take), *you cannot sell your liberty*.

To renounce liberty is to renounce being a man, to surrender the rights of humanity and even its duties. For him who renounces everything no indemnity is possible. Such a renunciation is incompatible with man's nature; to remove all liberty from his will is to remove all morality from his acts (SC I, IV, p. 8).

The formal conclusion of Chapter IV on alienation: total alienation is illegitimate and inconceivable because a contradiction in terms: 'incompatible with man's nature'.

And yet: it is this total alienation itself that constitutes the single clause of the Social Contract: 'the total alienation of each associate, together with all his rights, to the whole community.'

There can be no ambiguity: *liberty* is certainly included in 'all the rights' of each associate.

Let us stop a moment at this paradox. I can say: the total alienation of the Social Contract is the solution to the problem posed by the state of universal alienation that defines the state of war, culminating in the crisis resolved by the Social Contract. *Total alienation is the solution to the state of total alienation.*

Obviously, as I have already noted, Rousseau does not use the term alienation to designate the mechanism and effects of the state of war. Nevertheless I have shown that I am justified in using this anachronistic term to designate what Rousseau thinks of the nature of the state of war. The advantage of this substitution of terms is to make this conversion of sense, this change in the 'manner of existence', the sole solution offered to men, 'play' on a single concept: alienation.

Before the Contract, we are in the 'element' (in the Hegelian sense) of alienation without any external recourse. This alienation is the work of the very men who suffer it. The slavery of the state of war is a real alienation of man, forced to give his liberty for nothing in exchange for a pure illusion, that of believing himself to be free. We are certainly in the element of alienation: but it is unconscious and involuntary.

There is no solution to this total alienation except total alienation itself, but conscious and voluntary total alienation.

If this is indeed the case, we return in the solution itself to what I called the absolute limits to any possible solution. The solution cannot come from outside, and even within the world of alienation it cannot come from outside the single law governing that world. The solution is only possible on condition of 'playing' on the 'manner of existence' of this implacable law. It can only consist of returning in its origin to that law itself, total alienation, while 'changing its manner of existence', its modality. This is what Rousseau very consciously states elsewhere when he says that the remedy of the evil must be sought in its very *excess*. In a word, a forced total alienation must be turned into a free total alienation.

But the scandalous thing is as follows: how can a *total alienation* really be *free*, since we know from Chapter IV that this association of terms (alienation, liberty) is incompatible, an absolute contradiction? Hardly has it been glimpsed than the solution retreats into impossibility. The solution itself needs a solution.

This solution of the solution is contained in the Discrepancy between the Recipient Parties to the contract (Discrepancy I).

The Two Recipient Parties and their Discrepancy

Indeed, so far we have only examined one aspect of the Social Contract: what happens between the two Recipient Parties (RPs) in the form of total alienation. But who are these RPs?

On the one hand they are the individuals taken one by one, and on the other, the 'community'. Hence RP_1 = the individual, and RP_2 = the 'community'.

The contract is an act of exchange between the RP_1 and the RP_2. We know what the RP_1 *gives* in this act of exchange: *everything* (total alienation). But we do not yet know what is given by the RP_2.

RP_1 (individual) RP_2 (community)
(total alienation) ————→   ←———— (?)
                              (exchange)

If we ask, what will the RP_2 give? we run up against a 'minor' difficulty which we have ignored up till now: *who is the RP_2?* The 'community'. But what is the community? The union, the association of the individuals and their 'forces'. Is that not clear and adequate? And yet the whole mystery of the mechanism of the contract lies in the unique nature of this RP_2.

In a word, here is the difficulty: in every contract the two Recipient Parties exist prior to and externally to the act of the contract. In Rousseau's Social Contract, only the RP_1 conforms to these conditions. The RP_2 on the contrary, escapes them. It does not exist before the contract for a very good reason: it is itself the *product* of the contract. Hence the paradox of the Social Contract is to bring together two RPs, one of which exists both prior to and externally to the contract, while the other does not, since it is the product of the contract itself, or better: its object, its end. It is in this difference in theoretical status between the two Recipient Parties to the contract that we inscribe: *Discrepancy I.*

What is the community? Of whom is it composed? Of the same individuals who appear *as individuals* in the RP_1, i.e. at the other pole of the exchange. In the RP_2 they appear, too, but no longer as individuals, but all in their 'corporate capacity', i.e. in a different form, in a different 'manner of existence', precisely the form of a 'whole', of a 'union', and this is the community. This difference of 'form' is just a difference of form: the same individuals do appear in the two RPs. But it is not a 'minor' difference: it is the very *solution* of the contract inscribed in one of its *conditions:* the RP2.

Rousseau knows it, but it is symptomatic that he is content to reflect this singularity of the structure of the Social Contract by masking and *denegating* it in the very terms by which he signals it. Here are two examples.

In *Émile:*

The nature of the social pact is private and peculiar to itself, in that *the people only contracts with itself* (op. cit., p. 425).

Precisely: the people can only be said to 'contract with itself' by a *play on words*, on this occasion on the word that designates the RP1 as the 'people', a term only strictly applicable to the RP2, the community (the object of the contract being to think the act by which 'a people is a people').

And in the *Social Contract* itself:

This formula shows us that the act of association comprises a mutual understanding between the public and the individuals, and that *each individual, in making a contract, so to speak, with himself*, is bound in a double capacity; as a member of the Sovereign he is bound to the individuals, and as a member of the State to the Sovereign (SC I, VII, pp. 13–14).

Here the difference of 'form' which distinguishes between the RP1 and the RP2, in other words, the difference between the individual in the form of isolation and the individual in the form of the community, which defines the RP2, is thought in the category of individuality. The Discrepancy is admitted and at the same time negated in the '*so to speak*' of 'each individual in making a contract, so to speak, with himself . . . '.

To sum up:

The 'peculiarity' of the Social Contract is that it is an exchange agreement concluded between two RPs (like any other contract), but one in which the second RP does not pre-exist the contract since it is its product. The 'solution' represented by the contract is thus pre-inscribed in one of the very conditions of the contract, the RP2, since this RP2 is not pre-existent to the contract.

Thus we can observe in Rousseau's own discourse a Discrepancy within the elements of the contract: between the theoretical statuses of the RP1 and the RP2.

We also observe that Rousseau, aware of this Discrepancy, cannot but *mask* it with the very terms he uses when he has to note it: in fact he negates this Discrepancy, either by designating the RP1 by the name of the RP2 (the people), or the RP2 by the name of the RP1 (the individual). Rousseau is lucid, but he can do no other. He cannot renounce this Discrepancy, which is the very solution, in the shape of the procedure which inscribes this Discrepancy, not in the solution but in the conditions of the solution. That is why when Rousseau directly encounters this Discrepancy, he deals with it by denegation: by calling the RP1 by the name of the RP2 and the RP2 by the name of the RP1. Denegation is repression.

Thus this Discrepancy can be recognized between the content of the juridical concept of the contract, which Rousseau imports into his problematic to give it a cover, and the actual content of his contract. If we take as our point of reference the contract in its juridical concept, and if we argue that Rousseau takes it for the concept of the content which he gives us, we can say: Rousseau's contract does not correspond to its concept. In fact, his Social Contract is not a contract but an act of constitution of the Second RP for a possible contract, which is thus no longer the primordial contract. The Discrepancy between the Social Contract and its concept has the same content as the Discrepancy I have just defined. If the terms of the juridical contract in its concept are superimposed on the terms of Rousseau's Social Contract, a pertinent difference, a Discrepancy, emerges. It concerns the RP2.

One first conclusion can be drawn from these schematic remarks: it concerns the singular type of relation that there is between the juridical concept of the contract and the concept of the Social Contract. Why is Rousseau forced to think what he says in a concept which is not the concept of what he says? Why this recourse? Why this necessarily falsified recourse? What effects does Rousseau 'expect' from this falsified recourse. Or rather, to avoid the language of subjectivity, what effects necessarily call forth this recourse? These questions put us on the trail of the function fulfilled by that singular philosophical object, the Social Contract. This *Discrepancy* between the contract (borrowed from existing Law) and the artificial philosophical object of the Social Contract is not a difference in theoretical content pure and simple: every Discrepancy is also the index of an *articulation* in the *dis-articulation* constituted by the Discrepancy. In particular, an articulation of Rousseau's philosophy with existing Law by the intermediary of one of its real concepts (sanctioning a real practice), the contract, and with existing juridical ideology. The nature of the function fulfilled by Rousseau's philosophical thought can no doubt be elucidated by the study of the *articulations* which link it to the realities of Law, Politics, etc . . . , in the *dis-articulations* which, in the form of theoretical Discrepancies, constitute it as a *philosophy*, as *the* philosophy it is.

Another conclusion: if we consider this Discrepancy I, it is clear that, for perfectly objective reasons inscribed in the theoretical space of the 'play' it opens, it authorizes different 'readings' of Rousseau.

The 'plays' on *words* by which Rousseau himself negates the 'play' of the theoretical space opened by the Discrepancy, authorize, in the strong sense, the Kantian and Hegelian readings of the Social Contract. The 'play' on words which calls the RP2 by the name of the RP1 (the individual 'making a contract, so to speak, with himself') directly authorizes a Kantian reading of the Social Contract (cf. Cassirer). The 'play' on words which calls the RP1 by the name of the RP2 ('the people only contracts with itself') directly authorizes a Hegelian reading. In the first case, the contract is an anticipation of a theory of Morality, whose voice can be heard in certain already Kantian formulations (liberty as obedience to the law one has given oneself, etc.). In the second case, the contract is an anticipation of a theory of the Nation as a totality, a moment of the Objective Spirit which reveals its basic determinations on a number of occasions (the historical conditions of possibility of the contract, the theory of manners and morals, of religion, etc.). In both cases the philosophical object Social Contract is relieved of its primordial function. Neither Kantian Morality nor the Hegelian Nation are constituted by a 'contract'. Besides, is it not enough to *read* Rousseau closely to see that his Contract is not a contract?

And since I am dealing with the possible 'readings' of Rousseau – I do not know if it has already been attempted, but if it has not, it can certainly be foreseen – the Discrepancy allows a remarkable phenomenological (Husserlian) reading of the Contract, as a primordial *act of constitution* of the RP2, i.e. of the juridical community, in other words, as a primordial act of constitution of *juridical ideality* on the 'foundation' of the 'passive syntheses' of which the *Discourse on Inequality* gives us admirable descriptions, which only await their commentators.

Of course, the Discrepancy which thus makes objectively possible Kantian, Hegelian or Husserlian 'readings' of Rousseau also, thank God, makes possible a 'Rousseauist' reading of Rousseau. Better: without bringing to light and rigorously defining this Discrepancy, a 'Rousseauist' reading of Rousseau is impossible. For in order to read Rousseau in Rousseau, three things have to be taken into account: (1) the objective existence of this Discrepancy in Rousseau; (2) the denegation of this Discrepancy by Rousseau; and (3) the equally necessary character of the existence both of this Discrepancy and of its denegation, which do not arise as accidents in Rousseau's thought but *constitute* and *determine* it. To take into account this Discrepancy and its denegation is to take into account a theoretical fact, and its theoretical effects, which govern the whole logic of Rousseau's thought, i.e. both its possibility and its impossibilities, which are part of one and the same logic: that of a Discrepancy constitutive even in its denegation. If the Social Contract is not a contract but the (fictional) act of constitution of the Second Recipient Party (i.e. the *coup de force* of the 'solution'), in the same way it can be said that the Discrepancy is not what Rousseau says about it (its concept never being anything in Rousseau but the denegation of its *fait accompli*), but the act of constitution of Rousseau's philosophy itself, of its theoretical object and logic.

From here on it is clear that this logic can only be a *double* one: the logical chain of the problems thought being constantly inhabited by a second chain, the logical chain of the Discrepancies which follow them like their shadows, i.e. precede them as their arbitrary 'truth'.

Chapter Three

The Contract and Alienation

We can now return to total alienation. It was the solution, but an impossible because unthinkable one. Discrepancy I has made it possible, because thinkable.

If total alienation is possible, despite the contradiction of its concept, it is because of the nature of the Second Recipient Party: which features the same men as the RP1. It is possible because it is purely internal to the liberty of the individuals: it is possible because men give themselves totally, but to themselves.

To think Rousseau's novelty we must return to the classical contracts. In them, the two Recipient Parties are prior to the contract and different from one another: e.g. the People and the Prince. It follows that it is always a matter of a juridical contract of exchange: give and take. Not only is the contract an exchange, but if we try to apply the category of alienation to it, it turns out to be a *partial* alienation. The individual only cedes a part of his rights in exchange for his security (there is one exception: Hobbes, whom I shall discuss later). In Rousseau what is striking is the fact that the individual has to give everything, to give himself entirely, without any reserve, in order to receive something 'in exchange', even when exchange has no more meaning. Or rather: in order that the possibility of an exchange acquire a meaning, it is necessary that there be this initial total gift, which can be the object of no exchange. Hence Rousseau poses as *the* a priori *condition of any possible exchange this total alienation which no exchange will compensate*. The constitution of the Second Recipient Party, i.e. the community, is thus not an exchange but the constitution of the *a priori* condition of possibility of any (real or empirical) exchange. I shall return to this conclusion in a moment.

This theory of total alienation enables Rousseau to settle theoretically the 'terrifying' problem posed by the 'devil' Hobbes to all political philosophy (and to all philosophy as such). Hobbes's genius was to have posed the political problem with a merciless rigour in his theory of the state of war as a state, and to have claimed that the contract founding civil society was not a give-and-take contract of exchange between two Recipient Parties. Hobbes's contract, too, depends on a total alienation which the individuals agree among themselves to the advantage of a Third Party who is a Recipient in that he *takes everything* (absolute power), but is not a Recipient Party *to* the Contract since he is external to it and gives nothing in it. This Third Recipient Party, too, is constituted by the Contract, but as an effect external to the contract and its Recipient Parties (all the individuals contracting with one another to give everything to the Prince: it has been called a contract of donation, thinking of modern life-insurance contracts, i.e. to use a term which carries real weight with Hobbes, contracts of insurance against death). A total alienation in externality, to an external Third Party constituted by the Contract as an absolute Prince, this is Hobbes. Naturally, there are gaps in this 'system': what 'guarantee' is there against the despotism of a Prince who is not even bound by the exchange of a promise? How can one entrust oneself to his 'interests'? How is one to represent to him (and think) his 'duties'?

Rousseau's theoretical greatness is to have taken up the most frightening aspects of Hobbes: the state of war as a universal and perpetual state, the rejection of any transcendental solution and the 'contract' of total alienation, generator of absolute power as the essence of any power. But Rousseau's defence against Hobbes is to transform total alienation in externality into total alienation in internality: the Third Recipient Party then becomes the Second, the Prince becomes the Sovereign, which is the community itself, to which free individuals totally ₊alienate themselves without losing their liberty, since the Sovereign is simply the community of these same individuals. Finally, the rejection of any transcendence took, in Hobbes, the form of the factual transcendence of the Prince's externality to the contract. Rousseau is alone in remaining in immanence, without any recourse to a Third Party, even if it is a man. He accepts the law immanent in Hobbes's state of war: he only changes its *modality*.

Rousseau's advantage here is to be more 'Hobbesian' than Hobbes himself, and to retain the theoretical gains of Hobbes's thought. Rousseau's social body does indeed have all the categories of Hobbes's Prince. The community has all the attributes of a natural individual, but transposed into the 'element' of union: it is not a question here of a real individual (some man or some assembly which is the Prince) but of a moral totality, of the moral person constituted by the alienation of all the individuals. That power is in essence absolute, that it is inalienable, that it is indivisible, that it cannot 'err', all these scandalous theses of Hobbes's are repeated word for word by Rousseau, but converted to the new meaning conferred on them by the *internality of alienation*.

Let us consider only one of these theses: the essentially *absolute* character of any sovereign power (a 'philosopheme' which contains, in its order, the very principle of the Kantian conception of *a priori* conditions of possibility). The tiny but decisive difference separating Rousseau from Hobbes stares us in the face when Rousseau, who thinks in Hobbes, simultaneously thinks what he needs to protect himself from Hobbes's 'difficulties', in particular from the 'crux' of the 'guarantees' of the contract of alienation, which, in classical philosophy, inevitably takes the form of the problem of the *Third Man*. Indeed, if a conflict arises who will arbitrate between the People and the Prince? Hobbes's solution is to suppress the problem, but by suppressing the right to a guarantee. Hence obvious 'factual' difficulties. Rousseau confronts the problem without faltering. He too will suppress it, but without suppressing the right to a guarantee: by realizing it, which makes it superfluous. Hobbes certainly 'felt' that in order to suppress this problem, the contract would have to be no ordinary contract, the violation of which always requires the intervention of a third man, an arbiter – hence his contract of total alienation, but in externality which is merely to *transfer* the problem into the individuality of the Prince (his interest, his conscience, his duty). Rousseau's master-stroke is to see that a problem cannot be resolved simply by its suppression in a mere factual *transfer*, but only by really making it *superfluous*.

To suppose that a third man is required to arbitrate in a conflict between two R Ps to a contract is in fact to suppose that a third man outside the civil society of the contractors is required for that society to exist, and it is thus to suppose that civil society does not exist, since it leaves outside itself the very condition of its own existence: that third man. Hence it is to suppose that without saying so one is still in the element prior to the Social Contract, that principle is being settled by fact, the *a priori* conditions of all exchange by the empirical conditions of exchange, etc. The problem of the third man then becomes the index and proof that the political problem has been badly posed: the radical reduction which lays bare the *a priori* constitutive essence of the juridico-political has not been attained. In other words, to invoke the necessity for the third man is to admit that one is still in the element of violence and that one is still thinking the problems of civil society in the categories of the state of nature and the state of war.

In Rousseau's theory of total alienation this 'difficulty' disappears: there is no longer any need for an arbiter, i.e. for a third man, because, if I dare use the expression, *there is no Second Man*, because the Second Recipient Party is identical with the First, because for him individuals only ever contract with themselves, because the total alienation is for him purely internal. Between the individuals (subjects) and the Sovereign, there is no need for an arbiter, since the Sovereign is nothing but the union of the individuals themselves, existing as members of the Sovereign, in the 'form' of union.

Of what use is this new philosophical object, the Social Contract? For the 'resolution' of all these 'problems'. But the solution to these problems is never anything but the effectivity of Discrepancy I, which permits a non-contract to function as a contract, i.e. to make this Second Recipient Party, which is in fact the *solution* itself, appear to be one of its *conditions*. The 'true' problems are elsewhere: they must be pursued, for the effect of Discrepancy I is to 'chase' them constantly ahead of their supposed solution. Up to the point where it will be clear that the problems, which anyone might think at their beginnings, are really at an end, because their 'solution' was installed from the beginning, even before they appeared. Discrepancy is also inversion of sense.

Chapter Four

Total Alienation
and Exchange:
Discrepancy II

I was perhaps a little hasty in saying that the Social Contract was not a 'true' contract because it contained no exchange: total alienation excluding all possible exchange as a function precisely of its total character. And yet the Social Contract also functions as a juridical contract between two Recipient Parties: give and take. The individual gives everything – and receives nothing in exchange. The paradox of total alienation which appeared to us as this non-exchange, the condition of possibility of all exchange, does nevertheless produce an exchange. This is where I shall inscribe *Discrepancy II*.

Just as Rousseau noted Discrepancy I in remarking that the Social Contract was a contract of a 'private and peculiar' (*particulier*) type, he connotes Discrepancy II in the same way by saying that total alienation produces a 'peculiar' (*singulier*) effect:

> The peculiar fact about this alienation is that, in taking over the goods of individuals, the community, so far from despoiling them, only assures them legitimate possession, and changes usurpation into a true right and enjoyment into proprietorship. Thus the possessors ... have ... acquired, so to speak, all that they gave up (SC I, IX, p. 18).

I have started with the most astonishing, the most 'concrete' text, since it concerns the 'goods', the 'properties' of individuals. Note in passing a second '*so to speak*' (an index of the denegation of the Discrepancy, as in the previous case). This 'everything' that they give includes their goods. They give them, but to get them back as they gave them (except for the subtraction of taxes).

As they gave them? No: wearing the new 'form' of property, replacing mere possession. A particularly precise case of the change in 'manner of existence' produced by the Contract.

Another text is even more categorical:

Each man alienates, I admit, by the social compact, only such part of his powers, goods, and liberty as it is important for the community to control; but it must also be granted that the Sovereign is sole judge of what is important (SC II, IV, p. 24).

On this occasion the deduction is made within total alienation itself, i.e. the result of the exchange of alienation is shifted back onto it and then immediately removed from it. Hence: total alienation only applies to a part of that whole. How better express: it must be total so as not to be total. Discrepancy II.

We are really in the accountability of an exchange. Listen to Rousseau in SC I, VIII, p. 16. It is an accountable balance:

Let us draw up the whole account in terms easily commensurable. What man loses by the social contract is his natural liberty and an unlimited right to everything he tries to get and succeeds in getting; what he gains is civil liberty and the proprietorship of all he possesses. If we are to avoid mistake in weighing one against the other, we must clearly distinguish natural liberty, which is bounded only by the forces of the individual, from civil liberty, which is limited by the general will; and possession, which is merely the effect of force or the right of the first occupier, from property, which can be founded only on a positive title.

'Account', 'commensurable', 'loss', 'gain'. The language of accounts. The language of exchange. Result: the exchange is advantageous.

Thus we have both ends of the chain. On the one hand total alienation, on the other a real advantage. How can a total alienation be transmuted into an advantageous exchange? How can a total alienation, which could not receive anything in exchange that would be its equivalent, which appeared to us as the condition of possibility of all exchange, immediately and in itself take the form of an exchange, and even an advantageous one? What mechanism produces this astonishing effect?

This mechanism is a mechanism for the self-regulation, self-limitation of alienation, produced first on alienation itself by its total character. This mechanism is identical with the 'clauses' of the contract. If they have to be scrupulously respected without changing them one iota, this is in order to ensure the effect of the self-regulation and self-limitation of alienation itself.

'The clauses of this contract are so determined by the nature of the act that the slightest modification would make them vain and ineffective' (SC I, VI, p. 12).

What clauses? One formal clause: equality in total alienation. But also something which is not a clause, but a cause: *interest*.

Equality. Each gives *all* he is and has, whatever he has. All men are equal in alienation, since it is total for each of them. This is a formal clause, for men have unequal possessions, and we know that the exchange is advantageous to the one who possesses the most, for it is he who risks the greatest loss in the state of war.

Interest. This is what opens up the 'play' in the formal clause of equality, which *allows* interest to come into 'play'. 'The conditions are the same for all; and, this being so, no one has any interest in making them burdensome to others.' Why? Whoever wanted to make them 'burdensome to others' would make them burdensome to himself, automatically, as a function of the formal equality implied by total alienation. Hence it is certainly equality which plays the part of limitatory regulator even within total alienation. But this formal equality would be a dead letter were it not made active at each moment by the interest of each individual. The reciprocity of the contract lies in the formal equality produced by the total alienation. But this reciprocity would be empty and vain if the individual interest caught up in it did not really bring it into 'play'.

The undertakings which bind us to the social body are obligatory only because they are mutual; and their nature is such that in fulfilling them we cannot work for others without working for ourselves. Why is it that the general will is always in the right, and that all continually will the happiness of each one, unless it is because there is not a man who does not think of 'each' as meaning him, and consider himself in voting for all? This proves that equality of rights and the idea of justice which such equality creates originate in the preference each man gives to himself, and accordingly in the very nature of man. It proves that the general will, to be really such, must be general in its object as well as its essence; that it must both come from all and apply to all. . . . (SC II, IV pp. 24–5).

The matter is clear: behind rights, behind reciprocity, it is only ever a question of 'the preference each man gives to himself', of individuals who only 'think' of themselves, of 'working for themselves'. The mechanism of total alienation imposes on 'the preference for oneself', on the particular interest, a transformation whose end-result is, in one and the same movement, the production of the general interest (or general will) and the self-limitation of total alienation in partial alienation, or rather in advantageous exchange.

This is one of the points in Rousseau's theory which makes any Kantian 'reading' in terms of a morality thoroughly impossible. Strictly speaking, 'total alienation' might be taken for an expression designating the transcendence of the order of morality with respect to any interest. But total alienation produces its effects precisely only because it presupposes within it the determinant effectivity of interest. For Rousseau, interest (which is the form of self-respect in the system of social relations, state of war or contractual society) can never be 'put into parentheses' or 'transcended', except by itself. Without the effectivity of interest, there would be no self-regulation, no self-limitation of total alienation, nor its conversion into 'advantageous exchange'. It is because the interest of each individual is active in total alienation that each individual receives back what he gives and more besides. He will want for others what he wants for himself, as a function of the equality imposed by the clause of total alienation. But he would not want anything for others if he did not first want it for himself. The general interest is not the product of a moral conversion that tears the individual away from his interest: it is merely the individual interest forced into the generality of equality, limited by it but simultaneously limiting in its effects the total alienation which is the basis for this general equality.

Rousseau expounds the logic of this mechanism in the paragraphs of Chapter VI which immediately follow the exposition of the clause of total alienation. The last one sums them up:

Finally, each man, in giving himself to all, gives himself to nobody; and as there is no associate over which he does not acquire the same right as he yields over himself, he gains an equivalent for everything he loses, and an increase of force for the preservation of what he has (SC I, VI, p. 12).

This contract which is not an exchange thus paradoxically has an exchange as its effect. We now see why this total alienation can be both 'incompatible with man's nature' (SC I, IV, p. 8), and not contrary to it. In the Social Contract, man does not give himself completely for nothing. He gets back what he gives and more besides, for the reason that he only gives himself to himself. This must be understood in the strongest sense: he only gives himself to his own liberty.

We can now specify the nature of *Discrepancy II*. Discrepancy I lay in the difference in theoretical status of the two Recipient Parties, and in the fact that the Social Contract was not a contract of exchange, but the act of constitution of the Second Recipient Party.

What was 'chased away' at the first moment as a result of Discrepancy I reappears at the second moment in the form of Discrepancy II: the false contract functions as a true contract nonetheless, for it produces an *exchange*, and even more, an advantageous exchange. What had been 'chased away' at the first moment has now been 'caught up with' and thought at the second moment. But at the cost of *Discrepancy II: between total alienation and the exchange it produces*, between total alienation and the interest which ensures its self-limitation, self-regulation, by realizing this total alienation as an exchange.

But then we can go further: in the mechanism which inscribes the effectivity of the interest of each individual in the necessity of the universal (and hence egalitarian) form of total alienation, there is a Discrepancy of theoretical status, unthought, unassumed. In other words, it is not the same interest that produces the total alienation on the one hand and acts in it to realize it as an exchange on the other. This unthought 'problem' is 'chased away' and 'thrust aside'. The solution is itself a problem: the problem that Rousseau is to pose in the terms of particular interest and general interest (or particular will and general will). But already we suspect that this 'problem' itself can only be 'posed' on the condition of a new Discrepancy III.

To sum up: Discrepancy I concerns the difference between the RP1 and the RP2. Discrepancy II concerns the difference between total alienation and advantageous exchange. Discrepancy III is about to appear in the 'problem' of the general interest or general will, or, what amounts to the same thing, in the problem of the law.

Chapter Five

Particular Interest and General Interest, Particular Will and General Will:

Discrepancy III

All the remarks that follow presuppose a knowledge of the arrangement and nature of the Institutions that emerge from the Social Contract: the Sovereign (or legislature), the Government (or executive), the nature of the acts of the Sovereign (laws) and of the Government (decrees), and the subordinate relation of the Government to the Sovereign, for which it is no more than the 'official' or 'clerk'.

This arrangement reveals two orders of reality:

1. A basic, essential reality: it is on the side of the Social Contract and the Sovereign, on the side of the legislative power and law. There is the 'life' and 'soul' of the social body.

2. A secondary reality, whose whole essence it is to be delegation and execution, mission and commission: the Government and its decrees.

As a first approximation, the difference between these two orders of reality can be expressed in the statement that the essence of the former is *generality* and the essence of the latter *particularity*. Two categories which, in their distinction, dominate the whole 'nature', i.e. in fact all the theoretical 'problems', of the Social Contract. Let us look at this slightly more closely, examining the object *par excellence* which realizes the essence of the Sovereign: the law.

What is a law? The act proper to a Sovereign. What is its

essence? To be general: both in its form and in its content, as a decision of the general will, relating to a general object.

. . . when the whole people decrees for the whole people, it is considering only itself; and if a relation is then formed, it is between two aspects of the entire object, without there being any division of the whole. In that case the matter about which the decree is made is, like the decreeing will, general. This act is what I call a law (SC II, VI, p. 30).

And Rousseau adds: 'When I say that the object of laws is always general, I mean that law considers subjects as a body and actions in the abstract, and never a particular person or action.'

Let us consider this double generality of the law.

1. The generality of the law is the generality of its *form*: 'when *the whole people decrees* for the whole people'. The whole people = the entire people assembled together, *decreeing* for itself as a 'body', abstracting from the particular wills. The will of this body is the general will. Hence we can write: generality of the law = general will.

2. The generality of the law is the generality of its *object*: 'when the whole people decrees *for the whole people*'. The object of the law is the 'whole people', as a 'body' and considering only 'itself', abstracting from all particularity (action, individual). We can write: generality of the object of the law = general interest.

The unity of the law can then be written: *general will = general interest*.

This couple can only be explained by its opposite: *particular will = particular interest*. I think we know what particular will and particular interest are (cf. the *Discourse on Inequality*). The whole difficulty lies in understanding the generality of the will and of the interest as the same generality.

Rousseau's dream:

I should have wished to be born in a country in which the interest of the Sovereign and that of the people must be single and identical. . . . This could not be the case unless the Sovereign and the people were one and the same person ('Dedication' to the *Discourse on Inequality*).[1]

This dream is realized by the Social Contract, which gives

1. *The Social Contract and Discourses*, op. cit., p. 145.

Sovereignty to the assembled people. The act of legislation is indeed never anything but the Social Contract combined, repeated, and reactivated at each 'moment'. The primordial 'moment' which 'has made a people a people' is not a historical 'moment', it is the always contemporary primordial 'moment' which relives in each of the acts of the Sovereign, in each of his legislative decisions, the expression of the general will. But the general will only exists because its object *exists:* the general interest.

If the opposition of particular interests made the establishment of societies necessary, the agreement of these very interests made it possible. The common element in these different interests is what forms the social tie; and were there no point of agreement between them all, no society could exist. It is solely on the basis of this common interest that every society should be governed (SC II, I, p. 20).

We are now confronted with the problem of the relations between particular interest and general interest. But we have seen particular interest intervene in the very mechanism of the self-regulation of total alienation:

Why is it that . . . all constantly will the happiness of each one, unless it is because there is not a man who does not think of 'each' as meaning him, and consider himself in voting for all? This proves that equality of rights and the idea of justice which such equality creates originate in the *preference* each man gives to himself, and accordingly in the very nature of man (SC II, IV, pp. 24–5).

As a passage from the Geneva Manuscript (an early draft of the *Social Contract*) specifies, this *preference* is no more than another name for particular interest:

As the will tends towards the well-being of the wisher and the particular will always has as its object the private interest, the general will, the common interest, it follows that the last is or should be the only true motive force of the social body. . . , for the particular interest tends always to preferences and the public interest to equality.[2]

The paradox that springs from a comparison of these passages is the fact that the particular interest is presented both as the

2. Book I Chapter IV. Jean-Jacques Rousseau, *Oeuvres complètes* (Bibliothèque de la Pléiade), vol. III, p. 295. The last sentence is paraphrased in SC II, I, p. 20.

foundation of the general interest and as its opposite. To 'resolve' this contradiction, let us see how Rousseau treats it *practically* vis-à-vis the theoretical problem posed by the conditions of validity of *voting*.

In the people as a whole, in fact, voting has as its object the promulgation of laws, i.e. the declaration of the general will. How is one to proceed in order to know the general will? The principle is posed in SC IV, I, p. 86: '. . . the law of public order in assemblies is not so much to maintain in them the general will as to secure that the question be always put to it, and the answer always given by it.'

This passage means:

1. that the general will always exists, since it is, as the title of this chapter states, 'indestructible';

2. but that three conditions have to be brought into play for it to be able to declare itself.

It must first be asked a pertinent question, one which essentially relates to it: concerning not a particular object but a general object.

This question must be asked it in a pertinent form, one which really interrogates the general will itself and not the particular wills.

Lastly the general will must answer this question, i.e. existent as it is, it must not be 'mute', as happens when 'in every heart the social bond is broken'.

Supposing that a general question has been asked it, and that the general will is not mute, it must be interrogated in the forms required by its very nature if it is really to answer the question asked. This is the whole problem of voting rules:

The general will is always right and tends to the public advantage; but it does not follow that the deliberations of the people are always equally correct (SC II, III, p. 22).

In principle, the general will is the resultant of the particular wills:

. . . take away from these same wills the pluses and minuses that cancel one another, and the general will remains as the sum of the differences. . . . the grand total of the small differences would always give the general will (SC II, III, p. 23).

If such is the principle of the mechanism for the declaration of the general will, how can the deliberations of the people be incorrect and therefore fail to declare the general will? For the mechanism to carry out its function properly, two supplementary conditions are needed:

If, when the people, being furnished with adequate information, held its deliberations, the citizens had no communication one with another, the grand total of the small differences would always give the general will, and the decision would always be good (SC II, III, p. 23).

Hence the people must have 'adequate information', i.e. there must be 'enlightenment', which poses the problem of its political education.

But above all (and this is the decisive point) there must be no 'factions' or 'partial associations' in the State, above all no dominant partial association, for then what is 'declared' will no longer be the general will but a partial will, if not quite simply a particular will: that of the dominant group.

It is therefore essential, if the general will is to be able to express itself, that there should be no partial society within the State, and that each citizen should think only his own thoughts (SC II, III, p. 23).

An *absolute condition* for Rousseau: that the general will really is interrogated in its seat, in each isolated individual, and not in some or other group of men united by interests which they have in common, but which are still *particular* with respect to the general interest. If the general will is to declare itself, *it is thus essential to silence (suppress) all groups, orders, classes, parties, etc.* Once groups form in the State, the general will begins to grow silent and eventually becomes completely mute.

But when the social bond begins to be relaxed and the State to grow weak, when particular interests begin to make themselves felt and the smaller societies to exercise an influence over the larger, the common interest changes. . . . (SC IV, I, p. 85).

Note: the general will survives nonetheless, unalterable and correct: 'It is always constant, unalterable and pure; but it is subordinated to other wills which encroach upon its sphere.' The proof: in the most corrupt individual the general will is never destroyed, but only eluded.

The individual: 'Even in selling his vote for money, he does not extinguish in himself the general will, but only eludes it. The fault he commits is that of changing the state of the question, and answering something different from what he is asked. Instead of saying, by his vote, "It is to the advantage of the State," he says, "It is of advantage to this or that man or party that this or that view should prevail" ' (sc iv, i, p. 86).

We are now in a position to specify the nature and theoretical function of *Discrepancy III*.

I said: I think we know what particular interest is but we do not know what the general interest is. But Rousseau says that the general interest is the common ground of the particular interests. Each particular interest contains in it the general interest, each particular will the general will. This thesis is reflected in the proposition: that the general will is indestructible, inalienable and always correct. Which clearly means: the general interest always exists, the general will always exists, whether or no it is declared or eluded.

What separates the general interest from itself, the general will from itself? Particular interest. We have a total contradiction: particular interest is the essence of the general interest, but it is also the obstacle to it; now, the whole secret of this contradiction lies in a '*play*' on words in which Rousseau calls the *particular* interest of each individual in isolation and the *particular* interest of social groups *by the same name*. This second interest, which is a group, class or party interest, not the interest of each individual, is only called particular with respect to the general interest. It is a 'play' on words to call it particular in the way the interest of the isolated individual is called particular. This 'play' on words is once again the index of a Discrepancy: a difference in theoretical status of the isolated individual and social groups – this difference being the object of a denegation inscribed in the ordinary use of the concept of *particular interest*. This denegation is inscribed in so many words in his declaration of impotence: human groups must not exist in the State. A declaration of impotence, for if they *must not* exist, that is because they *do* exist. An absolute point of resistance which is not a fact of Reason but a simple, irreducible fact: the first encounter with a real problem after this long 'chase'.

But precisely the theoretical denegation, by the ambiguous use of one and the same concept ('particular interest'), of this 'resistant' fact allows the theory to develop without resistance, in the commentary on the mirror couple: particular interest/general interest. However, on closer inspection, we can see the Discrepancy at work even in this couple.

The general interest: its existence has as its sole content *the declaration of its existence*. Rousseau does not doubt for a moment the existence of a general interest as the foundation for every society. That the ideology of the general interest is indispensable to the real societies which served as references for Rousseau is certainly true. But in the *Social Contract*, Rousseau never treats the general interest as an ideology or myth. Its real existence is so little in doubt for him that he affirms its unalterable and imperturbable existence, even when the general will which declares it has become mute. Here the theoretical Discrepancy begins to reveal a quite different Discrepancy: the Discrepancy which installs this philosophy in the Discrepancy between it and the real which its birth required from the beginning.

The same is true, in mirror form, for the particular interest. For, the general interest is no more than the mirror reflection of the particular interest. The particular interest, too, is the object of an absolute *declaration of existence*. The two declarations echo one another since they concern the same content and fulfill the same function. And they are discrepant with respect to the same reality: the interests of social groups, the object of a denegation indispensable for the maintenance in working order of the mirror categories of particular interest and general interest. Just as the general interest is a myth, whose nature is visible once it is seen in demarcation from its real double, the 'general interests' which Rousseau calls 'particular' because they belong to human groups (orders, classes, etc.) – so the 'pure' particular interest of the isolated individual (what he obtains from the constitutive origins of the state of nature) is a myth, whose nature is visible once it is seen that it has a real 'double' in the general interests of human groups that Rousseau calls 'particular' because they dominate the State, or struggle for the conquest of its power. As in the previous cases, we can spot this Discrepancy, but only beneath the verbal denegation of a play on words: here the juggling with particular and general, concepts which properly belong exclusively to the individual and the Sovereign, but which serve theoretically to reduce the Discrepancy introduced into Rousseau's conceptual system by the emergence of the following irreducible phenomenon: the existence of the interests of social groups. The interest of these social groups is sometimes called particular, sometimes general, for the good of the Cause, the cause of the ideological mirror couple particular interest/general interest, which reflects the ideology of a class domination that presents its class interests to *particular* individuals as *their (general) interest*.

The Discrepancy now appears to us in all its breadth, and in a new form. It no longer concerns some or other point internal to the theory. It is no longer a question of the status of the Second Recipient Party (Discrepancy I) or of the status of the exchange in total alienation (Discrepancy II). This time it is a question of the very Discrepancy of the theory with respect to the real; for the first time the theory has encountered social groups in existence. Having reached this point, I can make one suggestion and one comment.

The suggestion. It would undoubtedly be very interesting to go back along the path we have just completed, but this time starting from Discrepancy III as the reason for all the earlier 'problems' and Discrepancies. That would be to start from the dis-articulation of Rousseau's philosophy, i.e. from the point at which it is articulated onto the juridical ideology of the society in which Rousseau lived, constituting itself as an ideological philosophy of politics by distancing itself through this Discrepancy III which constitutes it. By this procedure it could be demonstrated that the classical difference of and opposition between the external and internal criticism of a philosophical theory are mythical.

The comment. It is that in the object involved in the denegation of Discrepancy III (social groups, orders, classes, etc.), Rousseau has finally reached what he began with as a problem: the result of the *Discourse on Inequality*. And this comparison would no doubt give pertinent results for the ideological concepts underpinning all the theoretical space of the *Social Contract*: liberty, self-respect, equality, etc. The famous liberty in particular, solemnly attributed to the man of the first state of nature, the reserve and sacred depository for one-never-knows-how-long, i.e. for the Future of Morality and Religion (and for the General Will, i.e. for the General Interest) – it would become clear that the natural man has no need or use for it: that the whole of the *Discourse on Inequality* can quite well do without it. And it would also be seen what the social groups are all about: is it not the body of the 'rich' who take the initiative in the Social Contract, whose arguments are there denounced: the very 'deliberate' undertaking of the greatest imposture in the history of the human race? The true Social Contract, now a 'legitimate' one, thus finds at the end of the displacement of its concepts the very same realities whose existence and implacable logic had been described in the *Discourse on Inequality*.

One last comment. If Discrepancy III now concerns the Discrepancy of the theory with respect to the real, it can no longer be a question of a mere *theoretical* denegation. The *denegation* can only be a *practical one:* to denegate the existence of human groups (orders, classes) is to suppress their existence practically. Here I inscribe Discrepancy IV.

Chapter Six

Flight Forward in Ideology or Regression in the Economy:

Discrepancy IV

The solution to the existing 'theoretical difficulties' is entrusted to practice. It is a question of managing to suppress, in the reality which can no longer be avoided, the social groups and their effects: the existence of orders, of social classes, of political and ideological parties and of their effects.

Recall the conditions for the 'sound' functioning of the consultation of the general will. The people must be enlightened, and no intermediary human groups must be imposed between it and the general will. Rousseau will conduct the two tasks abreast, in one and the same operation, which takes two forms, the second being an avowal of the failure of the first, and vice versa. Flight forward in ideology and (or) regression in reality. Discrepancy IV, which is perfectly 'practical' (but naturally implies theoretical effects) 'separates' the two forms of this alternating attempt. Here I can only give a few brief indications.

I. THE FLIGHT FORWARD IN IDEOLOGY

The essential moments are to be found in the theory of manners and morals (*moeurs*), education and civil religion. In its principle this attempt has the aim of setting up the practical arrangements for a permanent moral reform intended to cancel out the effects of the social interest groups which are constantly arising and active in society. It is a question of ceaselessly defending and restoring the 'purity' of the individual conscience (i.e. of the particular interest which is in itself the general interest) in a society where it is threatened by the pernicious effects of 'particular' groups.

Listing the various sorts of laws, Rousseau distinguishes political laws, civil laws and criminal laws. But the essential remains unspoken:

Along with these three kinds of law goes a fourth, most important of all, which is not graven on tablets of marble or brass, but on the hearts of the citizens. This forms the real constitution of the State, takes on every day new powers, when other laws decay or die out, restores them or takes their place (*les supplée*), keeps a people in the ways in which it was meant to go, and insensibly replaces authority by the force of habit. I am speaking of morality (*moeurs*), of custom, above all of public opinion; a power unknown to political thinkers, on which none the less success in everything else depends. With this the Great Legislator concerns himself in secret, though he seems to confine himself to particular regulations; for these are only the arc of the arch, while manners and morals (*moeurs*), slower to arise, form in the end its immovable keystone (SC II, XII, pp. 44–5).

The cause in these unwritten key laws is the action on the 'particular will' which is embodied in the 'manners and morals'. 'Now, the less relation the particular wills have to the general will, that is, morals and manners to laws . . .' (SC III, I, p. 48). But the 'manners and morals' are no more than the penultimate link in the chain of a causality that can be depicted as follows:

Laws→public opinion→manners and morals→particular will

For their part, the social groups can be relied on to act automatically, by their mere existence as well as by their undertakings and influence, on each of the moments of this process. Hence it is indispensable that a counter-action be exercised on each of the intermediate causes. The Legislator acts *par excellence* on the laws. Education, festivals, civil religion, etc., on public opinion. The censors on manners and morals. But the Legislator only intervenes at the beginning of the historical existence of the social body, and the censors can only preserve good manners and morals, not reform bad ones. It is thus at the level of public opinion that action can and must be constant and effective. Hence the importance of the education of the citizens by public means (festivals) or private means (*Émile*): but education cannot be enough without recourse to religion, i.e. to religious ideology, but conceived as civil religion, i.e. in its function as a moral and political ideology.

Flight forward into ideology, as the sole means of protecting the particular will from the contagion of those so-called 'particular', i.e. social, 'interests' of the famous 'intermediary' groups. A flight forward: for it has no end. The ideological solution, that 'keystone' which holds up to heaven the whole political arc, needs heaven. Nothing is as fragile as Heaven.

2. REGRESSION IN (ECONOMIC) REALITY

That is why it is necessary to return to earth and to attack those dangerous human 'groups' in their very principles. And, remembering the main theses of the *Discourse on Inequality*, to speak of reality, i.e. of 'goods', of property, of wealth and of poverty. In clear terms: the State must be maintained in the strict limits of a definite economic structure.

. . . the end of every system of legislation . . . reduces itself to two main objects, *liberty* and *equality* – liberty, because all particular dependence means so much force taken from the body of the State, and equality, because liberty cannot exist without it. . . . By equality, we should understand, not that the degrees of power and riches are to be absolutely identical for everybody; but that power shall never be great enough for violence, and shall always be exercised by virtue of rank and law; and that, in respect of riches, no citizen shall ever be wealthy enough to buy another, and none poor enough to be forced to sell himself: which implies, on the part of the great, moderation in goods and position, and, on the side of the common sort, moderation in avarice and covetousness (SC II, XI, p. 42).

Here Rousseau adds a note:

If the object is to give the State consistency, bring the two extremes as near to each other as possible; allow neither rich men nor beggars. These two estates, which are naturally inseparable, are equally fatal to the common good;

from the one come the friends of tyranny, and from the other tyrants (SC II, XI, p. 42n.).

The central formulations of this passage repeat, but *vis-à-vis* their political effects, certain even of the terms of the *Discourse on Inequality*: 'From the moment one man began to stand in need of the help of another; from the moment it appeared advantageous to any one man to have enough provisions for two, equality disappeared.'[1] This possibility marks, with the beginning of the division of labour, the beginnings of dependence, which becomes universal when, all the land being cultivated and occupied, 'the supernumeraries . . . are obliged to receive their subsistence, or steal it, from the rich,'[2] and the rich are able to buy or constrain the poor. It is this reality which haunts the second practical solution of the *Social Contract*.

In the economic reforms he proposes, Rousseau aims to proscribe the effects of the established economic inequality, and especially the grouping of men into those two 'naturally inseparable' 'estates', 'rich men' and 'beggars'. The criterion he retains is that 'no citizen shall ever be wealthy enough to buy another, and none poor enough to be forced to sell himself'. He expresses out loud, but without thinking its practical preconditions, the old dream of economic independence, of 'independent commerce' (*Discourse on Inequality*), i.e. of (urban or agrarian) petty artisanal production.

'Flight backwards' this time, in economic reality: regression.

That it is a dream, a pious wish, is well known to Rousseau:

Such equality, we are told, is a speculative chimera which cannot exist in practice. But if its abuse is inevitable, does it follow that we should not at least make regulations concerning it? It is precisely because the force of circumstances tends continually to destroy equality that the force of legislation should always tend to its maintenance (SC II, XI, p. 42).

Clearly, it can only be a matter of regulating an inevitable abuse, an effect of the force of circumstances. When Rousseau

1. *The Social Contract and Discourses*, op. cit., p. 199.
2. ibid., p. 203.

speaks of 'bringing the two extremes as near to each other as possible', it is a question of the following impossible condition: to go against the force of circumstances, to propose as a practical measure a solution 'which cannot exist in practice'. It is hardly necessary to note that the two 'extremes' have all that is required to constitute themselves as human groups defending their 'interests' without caring a jot about the categories of generality or particularity.

In a word: Rousseau invokes as a practical solution to his problem (how to suppress the existence of social classes) an *economic regression* towards one of the phenomena of the dissolution of the feudal mode of production: the independent petty producer, the urban or rural artisanate, what the *Discourse on Inequality* describes in the concept of 'independent commerce' (universal economic independence permitting a 'free' commerce, i.e. free relations between individuals). But to what saint should one entrust oneself for the realization of this impossible regressive economic reform? There is nothing left but moral preaching, i.e. ideological action. We are in a circle.

Flight forward in ideology, regression in the economy, flight forward in ideology, etc. This time the Discrepancy is inscribed in the practice proposed by Rousseau. This practice concerns not concepts, but realities (moral and religious ideology which *exists*, economic property which *exists*). The discrepancy really is in so many words the Discrepancy of theory with respect to the real in its effect: a discrepancy between two equally impossible practices. As we are now in reality, and can only turn round and round in it (ideology-economy-ideology, etc.), there is no further flight possible in reality itself. End of the Discrepancy.

If there is no possibility of further Discrepancies – since they would no longer be of any use in the theoretical order which has done nothing but live on these Discrepancies, chasing before it its problems and their solutions to the point where it reaches the real, insoluble problem, there is still one recourse, but one of a different kind: a *transfer*, this time, the transfer of the impossible theoretical solution into the alternative to theory, literature. The admirable 'fictional triumph' of an unprecedented writing (*écriture*): *La Nouvelle Heloïse*, *Émile*, the *Confessions*. That they are unprecedented may be not unconnected with the admirable 'failure' of an unprecedented theory: the Social Contract.

Part Three

Marx's Relation to Hegel

I should like to thank Monsieur Jean Hyppolite for the great honour he has done me in inviting me to his Seminar. I am greatly indebted to M. Hyppolite. Among many other achievements, he will go down in the history of French philosophy as the man who has had the courage to translate Hegel and sponsor the publication of Husserl. He has pulled French philosophy away from the reactionary tradition which has dominated, I say *dominated* (for fortunately there have been other elements beneath this domination), its whole history since the French Revolution, a reactionary tradition reinforced by the academic reigns of Lachelier, Bergson and Brunschvicg. In this tradition French chauvinism took the form of the simplest kind of stupidity: ignorance. M. Hyppolite has had the courage to fight against this ignorance. We owe to him our knowledge of Hegel, and through Hegel, the beginnings of an understanding of, among other things, the distance separating Marx from Hegel. Let us not speak of the fate French philosophy has reserved for Marx. Brunschvicg, who thought Hegel mentally retarded, regarded Marx and Lenin as philosophical nonentities. M. Hyppolite has also had the courage to speak of Marx, and of Freud, those great *damnés de la terre* for academic bourgeois philosophy.

Everyone more or less knows this now. But it is worth saying.

Let me add that I have a debt to M. Hyppolite that he will not suspect. If I have been able to glimpse the revolutionary theoretical scope of Marx's work in philosophy, it is thanks to a very dear friend, Jacques Martin, who died five years ago. Now Jacques Martin was privileged, under the Occupation in Paris, to hear M. Hyppolite, then a *professeur de khâgne* (teacher in Letters in the preparatory class for the École Normale Supérieure), comment on certain passages from the *Phenomenology of Mind*.

From what I know of it, these were not, believe me, in that very special period, ordinary commentaries. What M. Hyppolite said then helped several of his students to orientate themselves 'in thought', as Kant put it, i.e. also in politics. M. Hyppolite has certainly forgotten the words he then uttered: but not everyone has forgotten them. I am here to bear witness. Against what common sense, the common sense of financiers and lawyers, tells us, there are many writings that blow away, but a few words that remain. No doubt because they have been inscribed in life and history.

I should like to put forward a few schematic themes about Marx's relation to Hegel.

I renounce rhetoric and maieutics, whether Socratic or phenomenological. In philosophy, the true beginning is the end. I shall begin at the end. I shall lay my cards on the table so every-one can see them. These cards are what they are: they carry the stamp of *Marxism-Leninism*. Exposed in this way, they will naturally have the form of a conclusion without premisses.

Let me start with a fact. The Marx-Hegel relationship is a currently decisive theoretical and political question. A *theoretical* question: it governs the future of the number-one strategic science of Modern Times: the science of history, and the future of the philosophy linked to that science: dialectical materialism. A *political* question: it derives from these premisses. It is in-scribed in the class struggle at a certain level, in the past as in the present.

To understand the contemporary importance of this fact of the Marx-Hegel relationship, it must be understood as a symptom, and explained as the symptom of the following realities. In order to situate the symptom, I shall state these realities in the form of *Theses*.

Thesis 1 (a statement of fact). *The union, or fusion of the Workers' Movement and Marxist theory* is the greatest event in the history of class societies, i.e. practically in all human history. Beside it, the celebrated great scientific–technical 'mutation' constantly resounding in our ears (the atomic, electronic, computer era, the space-age, etc.) is, despite its great importance, no more than a scientific and technical fact: these events are not of the same order of magnitude, they only bear in their effects on certain aspects of the productive forces, and not on what is decisive, the *relations of production.*

We are living in the necessary effects of this fusion, of this union. Its first results: the socialist revolutions (USSR, China, etc., revolutionary movements in Asia, Vietnam, Latin America, Communist Parties, etc.).

(a) This union realizes the 'union of theory and practice'.

(b) This union is not an established fact but an endless struggle, with its victories and defeats. A struggle in the union itself. With the 1914 War: the crisis of the Second International. At present: the crisis in the International Communist Movement.

The union brings together: the Workers' Movement and Marxist theory. Here I shall only discuss Marxist theory. What is Marxist theory?

Thesis 2 (a statement of fact). Marxist theory includes a science and a philosophy.

In the great classical tradition of the Workers' Movement, from Marx to Lenin, Stalin and Mao, Marxist theory has been defined as containing two distinct theoretical disciplines: a *science* (designated by its general theory: historical materialism) and a philosophy (designated by the term dialectical materialism). There are very special relations between these two disciplines. I shall not examine them in this paper. I shall suggest the following: of these two disciplines, science and philosophy, it is the science that has the place of determination (in the sense defined in *Reading Capital* and closely specified by Badiou in *Critique*, May 1967).[1] *Everything depends on this science.*

1. 'Le (Re)-commencement du matérialisme dialectique', *Critique*, no. 240, May 1967.

Thesis 3. <u>Marx founded a new science: the *science of the history*</u> <u>of social formations, or the science of history.</u>

The foundation of the science of history by Marx is the most important theoretical event of contemporary history.

Let me use an image.

There are a certain number of sciences. They can be said to occupy a certain site in what can be called a theoretical space. Site, space. Metaphorical notions. But they convey certain facts: the proximity of certain sciences; relations between neighbouring sciences; domination of certain sciences over other sciences; but simultaneously sciences without neighbours, insular sciences (isolated positions in a void: e.g. psychoanalysis, etc.).

From this standpoint it is possible to consider that the history of the sciences reveals the existence, in this problematical theoretical space, of *great scientific continents*.

1. The continent of Mathematics (opened up by the Greeks).

2. The continent of Physics (opened up by Galileo).

3. Marx has opened up the third great continent: the continent of History.

A continent, in the sense of this metaphor, is never empty: it is always already 'occupied' by many and varied more or less ideological disciplines which do not know that they belong to that 'continent'. For example, before Marx, the History continent was occupied by the philosophies of history, by political economy, etc. The opening-up of a continent by a continental science not only disputes the rights and claims of the former occupants, it also completely restructures the old configuration of the 'continent'. A metaphor cannot be spun out indefinitely – otherwise I should here say that the opening-up of a new continent to scientific knowledge presupposes a *change of terrain* or an *epistemological* 'rupture', etc. I leave you the trouble of the temporary needlework required to bring all these metaphors into agreement. But one day we shall have to drop all this sewing and patching for something quite different: to make a theory of the history of the production of knowledges.

Thesis 4. Every great scientific discovery induces a great transformation in philosophy. The scientific discoveries which open up the great scientific continents constitute the major dates in the *periodization* of the history of philosophy:

1st continent (Mathematics): birth of philosophy. Plato.

2nd continent (Physics): profound transformation of philosophy. Descartes.

3rd great continent (History, Marx): revolution in philosophy, announced in the 11th Thesis on Feuerbach. End of classical philosophy, no longer an interpretation of the world, but a '*transformation*' of the world.

'Transformation of the world': an enigmatic word, prophetic but enigmatic. How can philosophy be a transformation of the world? of which world?

Whatever the case, it is possible to say, with Hegel: philosophy always arrives *post festum*. It is always *late*. It is always *postponed* (*différée*).

This thesis is very important to me: in a certain respect (its theoretical elaboration), Marxist philosophy or dialectical materialism *cannot but be behind the science of history*. Time is needed for a philosophy to form and then develop after the great scientific discovery which has silently induced its birth.

All the more so in that, in Marx's case, the scientificity of his discovery has been fiercely denied, fought and condemned by all the self-styled specialists of that continent. The so-called Human Sciences still occupy the old continent. They are now armed with the latest ultra-modern techniques of mathematics, etc., but they are still based theoretically on the same outworn ideological notions as they were in the past, ingeniously rethought and retouched. With a few remarkable exceptions, the prodigious development of the so-called human sciences, above all the development of the social sciences, is no more than the *aggiornamento* of old techniques of social adaptation and social readaptation: of *ideological* techniques. This is the great scandal of the whole of contemporary intellectual history: everyone talks about

Marx, almost everyone in the human or social sciences says he is more or less a Marxist. But who has taken the trouble to read Marx closely, to understand his novelty and take the theoretical consequences? Without exception, the specialists of the human sciences one hundred years after Marx work with outdated ideological notions like Aristotelean physicists carrying on with Aristotelean physics fifty years after Galileo. Where are the philosophers who do not take Engels and Lenin for philosophical nonentities? I believe thay can be counted on the fingers of one hand. Not all Communist philosophers even, far from it, think well of Engels and Lenin as 'philosophers'. Where are the philosophers who have studied the history of the workers' movement, the history of the 1917 Revolution and the Chinese Revolution? Marx and Lenin have the great honour to share the fate of intellectual pariah with Freud and to be travestied when they are discussed as he is travestied. This scandal is not a scandal: the relations that reign between philosophical ideas are what are called relations of forces, ideological, and therefore political relations of forces. But it is bourgeois philosophical ideas that are in power. The question of power is the number-one question in philosophy, too. Philosophy is indeed in the last instance *political*.

Thesis 5. How is Marx's scientific discovery to be *explained*?

If we take seriously what Marx tells us about the real dialectic of history, it is not 'men' who make history, although its dialectic is realized in them and in their practice, but the masses in the relations of the class struggle. This is true for political history, general history. For the history of the sciences, making due allowances, the same is true. It is not individuals who make the history of the sciences, although its dialectic is realized in them, and in their practice. The empirical individuals known for making such and such a discovery realize in their practice *relations* and a *conjunction* wider than themselves.

This is where we can pose the problem of the relations between Marx and Hegel.

I shall give an extraordinarily schematic figuration. I hope it will be taken only for what it is: the index of a problem, and the indication of the schematic conditions for it to be *posed*.

To pose it thus in outline, I shall start once again from an indication of Engels's, taken up and developed by Lenin and known by the name of the Three Sources of Marxism. *Sources* is an outdated ideological notion, but what matters to us is the fact that Engels and Lenin do not pose the problem in terms of an individual history, but in terms of a *history of theories.* They establish a pattern involving three theoretical 'characters': Classical German Philosophy, English Political Economy and French Socialism. Say: Hegel, Ricardo and Babeuf-Fourier, Saint-Simon, etc. To simplify and for expositional clarity, I shall partially set aside French Socialism and consider only Ricardo and Hegel, as symbolic representatives of English political economy and German philosophy respectively.

I shall then return to the *extremely* general diagram of 'theoretical practice' which I proposed five years ago in an article on the *Materialist Dialectic.*

Diagram I

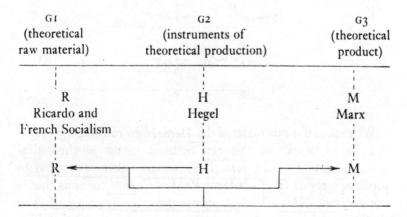

G1 (theoretical raw material)	G2 (instruments of theoretical production)	G3 (theoretical product)
R Ricardo and French Socialism	H Hegel	M Marx
R ←	H	→ M

Which means very schematically that Marx (*Capital*) is the product of the work of Hegel (German Philosophy) on English Political Economy + French Socialism, in other words, the *Hegelian dialectic* on: *Labour theory of value* (R) + *the class struggle* (FS).

R+FS = raw material, object of Marx's theoretical practice

H = instruments of theoretical production,

the product of the work of the Hegelian dialectic on Ricardo is then *Capital* = M.

[What we tried to do in *Reading Capital* can be represented, in thoroughly indicative fashion, by the following diagram:

Diagram II

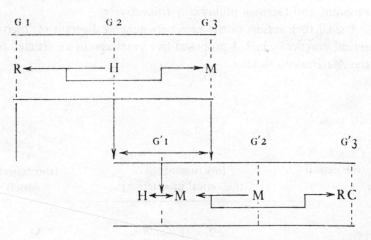

We took as our raw material the *Marx-Hegel* relationship (G′1). We set to 'work' on this raw material means of theoretical production G′2 (Marx himself + certain other categories) to produce a result G′3: whatever *Reading Capital* contains that is not aberrant. This labour is provisional – for us above all. The theoretical labour process *must be pursued* in a new cycle in which G′2 might be represented by the (+ or — erroneous) relation between Marx and *Reading Capital*, etc. Experience has very quickly shown that it is impossible to hold to this *internal* circle: the only way to advance is via the experience of the class struggle.]

Let us return to Diagram I. *Capital* is the product of the work of the Hegelian dialectic on Ricardo, etc.

This is a perfectly classical thesis, and one which can, of course, equally well support orthodox-Marxist as anti-Marxist interpretations, since in its schematic formulation, this thesis can give weight to the idea that Marx's relation to Ricardo is reducible to a relation of the *application* of Hegel to Ricardo.

However, this thesis is always stated in the classical tradition along with another equally, if not more, insistent one: the thesis of the *inversion*. It is not Hegel that is applied to Ricardo but Hegel inverted. An enigmatic expression. What does *inversion* mean? The first index of a problem.

A second index. Very many examples can be found in the classics of Marxism. I shall only take one: Lenin's paradoxical and apparently contradictory declarations on the Marx-Hegel relationship.

In *What the 'Friends of the People' are*, Lenin says that Marx has nothing to do with Hegelian triads and that *Capital* is not their application to Ricardo.

But in his *Reading Notes* (known as the *Philosophical Notebooks*), Lenin writes: 'Aphorism: *it is impossible completely to understand Marx's* Capital, *and especially its first chapter, without having thoroughly studied and understood the whole of Hegel's* Logic. *Consequently, half a century later none of the Marxists understood Marx*!!'.[2]

However, a page earlier in the same notes, Lenin writes: '*Hegel's analysis of syllogisms . . . recalls Marx's imitation of Hegel in Chapter One.*'[3]

An expression notably recalling a famous and enigmatic expression of Marx, who, in the Afterword to the second German edition of *Capital*, says: 'Just as I was working at the first volume

2. Lenin, *Collected Works*, vol. 38 (London and Moscow, 1961), p. 180.
3. ibid., p. 178.

of "Das Kapital", it was the good pleasure of the peevish, arrogant, mediocre *epigonoi* who now talk large in cultured Germany, to treat Hegel in same way as the brave Moses Mendelssohn in Lessing's time treated *Spinoza*, i.e. as a "dead dog". I therefore openly avowed myself the pupil of that mighty thinker, and even *here and there*, in the chapter on the theory of value, *coquetted (kokettieren) with the modes of expression peculiar to him. . . .*'

A strange application of Hegel to Ricardo. Let me sum up:

1. Not Hegel: but Hegel *inverted*. Inversion = rational kernel extracted from its mystical shell.

2. Further: 'coquetting' with Hegelian modes of expression (says Marx); an 'imitation' (says Lenin).

3. Leaving aside the imitation and coquettry, there remains the strange inversion. It is the inversion of idealism into materialism: matter in place of the idea. But to say this is to be much too general with respect to what is in question. For Feuerbach had already said and done just this, *in ideology*. Now, our inversion does not only concern the general world outlook but one very precise point: the *dialectic*. Marx 'inverts' it, for his dialectic is the 'direct opposite' of the Hegelian dialectic. What is the opposite of the Hegelian dialectic? A mystery. We must go further: to the *rational kernel*, i.e. to a content with a scientific theoretical value. Then it is no longer a matter of inversion but one of *critical extraction*, of a 'demystification' of the dialectic. What is a demystification? There is no longer any question of an application.

I have brought these indices together and, with considerable difficulty and at the cost of much clumsiness, have advanced the following hypothesis:

1. Marx did not 'apply' Hegel to Ricardo. He made something from Hegel *work* on Ricardo.

2. This something from Hegel is first Hegel *inverted*. The inversion of Hegel only concerns his *world outlook* = the inversion of idealism into materialism. World outlook = *tendency*. Nothing more: the tendency of a World Outlook does not *ipso facto* provide any scientific concepts.

3. This something from Hegel is thus something quite different from the *inversion* of the idealist tendency into the materialist tendency. It is something which concerns the *dialectic*. Here the metaphor of the inversion ceases to serve any useful purpose: it is replaced by a different metaphor. To invert the Hegelian dialectic = to demystify it = to *separate* the rational kernel from the irrational shell. This separation is not a mere sorting out: (take some and leave some). It can only be a transformation. Marx's dialectic can only be the Hegelian dialectic worked-transformed.

4. Thus Marx makes Hegel work on Ricardo: he makes a transformation of the Hegelian dialectic work on Ricardo.

It is indeed necessary to say that the Hegelian dialectic has been *transformed* in the theoretical work it has carried out on Ricardo. The theoretical instrument of labour which transforms the theoretical raw material is itself transformed by its work of transformation.

The result is the dialectic at work in *Capital : it is no longer the Hegelian dialectic but a quite different dialectic.*

We took this difference for the raw material of our work, as I have suggested in *Diagram II.*

Hence the results that appear in *For Marx* and *Reading Capital.*

Essentially we found in Marx:

— A non-Hegelian conception of *history.*
— A non-Hegelian conception of the *social structure* (a structured whole in dominance).
— A non-Hegelian conception of the *dialectic.*

Hence, if these theses are well-founded, they have crucial consequences for philosophy: above all, the rejection of the basic system of classical philosophical categories.

This system can be written:

(Origin = ((Subject = Object) = Truth) = End = Foundation)

This system is circular, because the Foundation is the fact that the adequation of subject and object is the teleological origin of all truth. I cannot justify this circular sequence here.

There follows from this rejection a new conception of philosophy – not only a new conception – but a new modality of existence, I shall say a new *practice* of philosophy: a philosophical discourse that speaks *from somewhere else* than classical philosophical discourse did. To make this comprehensible, let me invoke the analogy of psychoanalysis.

1. The point is to carry out a *displacement* = to make something *move over* (*bouger*) in the internal disposition of the philosophical categories.

2. Such that philosophical discourse changes its *modality* – speaks *otherwise* (*autrement*), which creates the difference between interpreting the world and changing it.

3. Without philosophy disappearing nonetheless.

Apparently it is the most conscious discourse there is. *In fact* it is the discourse of an *unconscious*. The point is no more to suppress philosophy than it would be to suppress the unconscious in Freud. What is required is, by working on the phantasms of philosophy (which underly its categories), to make something move over in the disposition of the instances of the philosophical Unconscious, so that the unconscious discourse of philosophy finds its *site* – and speaks at the top of its voice about the very *site* assigned to it by the instances which produce it.

I shall leave these crucial questions here.

One point remains. Everything we have published on Hegel in fact leaves out the positive heritage Marx, by his own confession, owed to Hegel. Marx transformed the Hegelian dialectic, but he owed Hegel a crucial gift: *the idea of the dialectic*. We have not discussed this. I should like to say a little about it.

In the Afterword to the second German edition of *Capital*, Marx discusses the dialectic in the following terms: '. . . The mystification which the dialectic suffers in Hegel's hands, by no means prevents him from being the first to present (*darstellen*) its general form of motion in a comprehensive and conscious manner. With him it is standing on its head. It must be turned right side up again, if you would discover the rational kernel within the mystical shell.

'In its mystified form, the dialectic became the fashion in

Germany, because it seemed to transfigure the existing state of things (*das Bestehende*). In its rational shape (*Gestalt*) it is a scandal and abomination to bourgeoisdom and its doctrinaire spokesmen, because it includes in the positive comprehension of the existing state of things at the same time also the comprehension of the negation of that state, of its inevitable breaking up; because it regards every developed form as in fluid movement and thus takes into account its transient nature, lets nothing impose upon it, and is in its essence critical and revolutionary.'[4]

Two notions stand out in this passage:

1. The dialectic is critical and *revolutionary*.

Now, the ambiguity of the dialectic is clear. It can be

(a) either a *transfiguration* of the existing state of things, the '*fait accompli*' (*das Bestehende*), the existing order. The dialectic: benediction of the existing order (social, scientific).

(b) or *critical and revolutionary*: it implies the *relativity* of every established order, social and theoretical, of societies and of systems, of institutions and of concepts.

The dialectic: a critique of the absolute by historical relativism.

This theme is very clear in Engels: the dialectic sets concepts in motion. A direct adoption of the Hegelian theme: *Reason* as a critique of the *Intellect*. Reason sets the concepts of the Intellect in motion.

The classical opposition in Marxism between

$$\left.\begin{array}{l}\text{metaphysical materialism} \\ \text{dialectical materialism}\end{array}\right\} = \begin{array}{l}\text{metaphysical/dialectical} \\ \text{opposition}\end{array}$$

is thus no more than the adoption of the Hegelian opposition between *Intellect* and *Reason*.

Stop at this and one has not yet left Hegel. It is still very formal and thus very dangerous. The proof: the spontaneously relativist/ historicist interpretation of this conception of the dialectic as a critique of the fixity of the intellect. Counterproof: Lenin's vigorous reaction against relativism and historicism (*Materialism and Empirio-Criticism*), bourgeois ideologies of history and of the dialectic.

4. *Capital*, vol. I (Moscow, 1961), p. 20.

2. But there is something else of much greater importance: does the Hegelian *dialectic* contain a *rational kernel* – and if so, what is it?

To see this, a *long detour* is required. It is necessary to go back through Marx's theoretical history. The decisive moment in this history is the rupture with *Feuerbach*. This rupture is announced in the lightning flash of the Theses on Feuerbach. The Theses on Feuerbach were written in haste after a crucial theoretical event: *the introduction of Hegel into Feuerbach* (it took place in the *1844 Manuscripts*). The *Manuscripts* are an *explosive* text. Hegel, re-introduced by force into Feuerbach, induces a prodigious *acting out* of the Young Marx's theoretical contradiction, in which is achieved the rupture with Theoretical Humanism.

To speak of Marx's rupture with Theoretical Humanism is a very precise thesis: if Marx broke with this ideology, that means he had espoused it; if he had espoused it (and it was no un-consummated marriage) that means it existed. The Theoretical Humanism Marx espoused was that of Feuerbach.

Marx 'discovered' Feuerbach, like all the Young Hegelians, in very special conditions, which I have said something about, following Auguste Cornu. For a time Feuerbach 'saved' the young Hegelian radicals theoretically from the insoluble contradictions induced in their liberal-rationalist 'philosophical conscience' by the obstinacy of the damned Prussian State, which, being 'in itself' Reason and Freedom, persisted in misrecognizing its own 'essence', persevering beyond all propriety in the Unreason of Despotism. Feuerbach 'saved' them theoretically by providing them with the reason for the Reason-Unreason contradiction: by a theory of the *alienation of Man*.

Obviously it would be impossible, on whatever basis, even a Marxist one, to think that the matter of Feuerbach can be settled by a confessional note of the kind: a few quotations from him, or from Marx and Engels, who *had* read him. Nor is it settled by that adjective of convenience and ignorance which nonetheless resounds in so many disputes: a *speculative* anthropology. As though it were enough to remove the speculation from the anthropology for the anthropology (assuming one knows what that word designates) to stand up: cut the head off a duck and it won't go far. As though it were also enough to pronounce these magic words to call Feuerbach by his name (philosophers, even if they are not watchdogs, are like you and me: for them to come, they must at least be called *by their names*). Let me therefore try to call Feuerbach by his name, even if need be by an abbreviation of his name.

Of course, I shall only discuss the Feuerbach of the years 1839–45, i.e. the author of *The Essence of Christianity* and the *Principles of the Philosophy of the Future* – and not the post-1848 Feuerbach, who, against his own earlier precepts, put a lot of 'water in his wine' for fear of the (1848) Revolution.

The Feuerbach of *The Essence of Christianity* occupies a quite extraordinary position in the history of philosophy. Indeed, he brings off the *tour de force* of putting an 'end to classical German philosophy', of overthrowing (to be quite precise: of 'inverting') Hegel, the Last of the Philosophers, in whom all its history is summed up, by a philosophy that was *theoretically retrogressive* with respect to the great German idealist philosophy.

Retrogressive must be understood in a precise sense. If Feuerbach's philosophy carried in it traces of German idealism, its theoretical foundations date from *before* German idealism. With Feuerbach we return from 1810 to 1750, from the nineteenth to the eighteenth century. Paradoxically, for reasons that should make a good 'dialectic' derived from Hegel giddy, it was by its *retrogressive* character in theory that Feuerbach's philosophy had fortunate progressive effects in the ideology, and even in the political history, of its partisans. But enough on this.

A philosophy which carries *traces* of German idealism but which settles accounts with German idealism, and its supreme representative, Hegel, by a *theoretically retrogressive* system, what are we to make of that?

The *traces* of German idealism: Feuerbach takes up the philosophical problems posed by German idealism. Above all the problems of Pure Reason and Practical Reason, the problems of Nature and Freedom, the problems of Knowledge (what can I know ?), of Morality (what ought I to do ?) and of Religion (what can I hope for ?). Hence Kant's fundamental problems, but 'returned to' via Hegel's critique and solutions (broadly the critique of Kantian distinctions as abstractions, which for Hegel derive from a misrecognition of Reason reduced to the role of the Intellect). Feuerbach poses the problems of German idealism with the intention of giving them a Hegelian type of solution: indeed, he tries to pose the *unity* of the Kantian *distinctions* or *abstractions* in something resembling the Hegelian Idea. This 'something' resembling the Hegelian Idea, while being its radical *inversion*, is *Man*, or *Nature*, or *Sinnlichkeit* (simultaneously sensuous materiality, receptivity and sensuous intersubjectivity).

To hold all this together, I mean to think as a *single* unit these three notions: Man, Nature and *Sinnlichkeit*, is a dumbfounding theoretical gamble, which makes Feuerbach's 'philosophy' a philosophical velleity, i.e. an actual theoretical inconsistency invested in a 'wish' for an impossible philosophical consistency. A moving 'wish', certainly, even a pathetic one, since it expresses and proclaims in great solemn cries the desperate will to escape from a philosophical ideology against which it remains definitively a rebel, i.e. its prisoner. The fact is that this impossible unity gave rise to a work which has played a part in history and produced disconcerting effects, some immediate (on Marx and his friends), others postponed (on Nietzsche, on Phenomenology, on a certain modern theology, and even on the recent 'hermeneutic' philosophy which derives from it).

It was an impossible unity (Man-Nature-*Sinnlichkeit*) which enabled Feuerbach to 'resolve' the great philosophical problems of German idealism, 'transcending' Kant and 'inverting' Hegel. For example, the Kantian problems of the distinction between Pure Reason and Practical Reason, between Nature and Freedom, etc., find a solution with Feuerbach in a *unique* principle: Man and his attributes. For example, the Kantian problem of scientific objectivity, and the Hegelian problem of religion find a solution with Feuerbach in an extraordinary theory of *mirror* objectivity ('the object of a being is the objectification of its Essence': the object – the objects – of Man are the objectification of the Human Essence). For example, the Kantian problem of the Idea and History, transcended by Hegel in the theory of the Spirit as the ultimate moment of the Idea, finds a solution with Feuerbach in an extraordinary theory of the intersubjectivity constitutive of the human species. As the principal term in all these solutions, we always find Man, his attributes, and his 'essential' objects (mirror 'reflections' of his Essence).

Thus, with Feuerbach, Man is the unique, primordial and fundamental concept, the *factotum*, which stands in for Kant's Transcendental Subject, Noumenal Subject, Empirical Subject and Idea, which also stands in for Hegel's Idea. The 'end of classical German philosophy' is then quite simply a verbal suppression of its solutions which respects its problems. It is a replacement of its solutions by heteroclite philosophical notions gathered from here and there in the philosophy of the eighteenth century (sensualism, empiricism, the materialism of *Sinnlichkeit*, borrowed from the tradition of Condillac; a pseudo-biologism vaguely inspired by Diderot; an idealism of Man and the 'heart' drawn from Rousseau), and unified by a *play on theoretical words* within the concept of Man.

Hence the extraordinary position and the effects Feuerbach could draw from his inconsistency: declaring himself in turn and all at once (and he saw no malice or inconsistency in it himself) a materialist, an idealist, a rationalist, a sensualist, an empiricist, a realist, an atheist and a humanist. Hence his declamations against Hegel's speculation, reduced to *abstraction*. Hence his appeals to the concrete, to the 'thing itself', to the real, to the sensuous, to matter, against all the forms of alienation, whose ultimate essence is for him constituted by *abstraction*. Hence the sense of his 'inversion' of Hegel, which Marx long espoused as the real critique of Hegel, whereas it is still entirely trapped in the empiricism of which Hegel is no more than the sublimated theory: to invert the attribute into the subject, to invert the Idea into the sensuous real, into matter, to invert the Abstract into the Concrete, etc. All that within the category of *Man*, who is the Real, the

Sensuous, and the Concrete. An old tune whose worn-out variations are still served up for us today.

There you have the *Theoretical Humanism* which Marx had to deal with. I say *theoretical*, for Man is not just for Feuerbach an Idea in the Kantian sense, but the theoretical foundation for *all* his 'philosophy', as the Cogito was for Descartes, the Transcendental Subject for Kant and the Idea for Hegel. It is this Theoretical Humanism that we find in so many words in the *1844 Manuscripts*.

But before turning to Marx, one more word on the consequences of this paradoxical philosophical position which claims radically to abolish German idealism but which respects its problems and hopes to resolve them by the intervention of a heap of eighteenth century concepts, gathered together within the theoretical injunction of Man, which stands in for their 'philosophical' unity and consistency.

For it is not possible to 'return' with impunity to a position *behind* a philosophy while retaining the problems it has brought to light.

The fundamental consequence of this theoretical retrogression accompanied by a retention of current problems is to induce an enormous *contraction* of the existing philosophical problematic, behind the appearances of its 'inversion', which is no more than the impossible 'wish' to invert it.

Engels and Lenin were perfectly well aware of this 'contraction' with respect to Hegel. 'Feuerbach is small in comparison with Hegel.' Let us go straight to the essential: what Feuerbach unforgiveably sacrificed of Hegel is History and the Dialectic, or rather, since it is one and the same thing for Hegel, History *or* the Dialectic. Here too, Marx, Engels and Lenin made no mistake: Feuerbach is a materialist in the sciences, but . . . he is an idealist in History. Feuerbach speaks of Nature but . . . he does not speak of History – Nature standing in for it. Feuerbach is not dialectical. Etc.

Having obtained this perspective, let us specify these established judgements.

Of course, history certainly is discussed by Feuerbach, who hopes to distinguish between the 'Hindu', the 'Judaic', the 'Roman', etc., 'human natures'. But there is no *theory* of history in his work. And above all there is no trace of the theory of history we owe to Hegel as *a dialectical process of production of forms* (*figures*).

Of course, as we can now begin to say, what irremediably disfigures the Hegelian conception of History as a dialectical process is its *teleological* conception of the dialectic, inscribed in the very *structures* of the Hegelian dialectic at an extremely precise point: the *Aufhebung* (transcendence-preserving-the-transcended-as-the-internalized-transcended), directly expressed in the Hegelian category of the *negation of the negation* (or negativity).

To criticize the Hegelian philosophy of History because it is *teleological*, because from its origins it is in pursuit of a goal (the realization of Absolute Knowledge), hence to reject the teleology in the philosophy of history, but to return to the Hegelian dialectic as such at the same time, is to fall into a strange contradiction: for the Hegelian dialectic, too, is teleological in its *structures*, since the key structures of the Hegelian dialectic is the *negation of the negation, which is the teleology itself*, within the dialectic.

That is why the question of the structures of the dialectic is the key question dominating the whole problem of a materialist dialectic. That is why Stalin can be taken for a perceptive Marxist philosopher, at least on this point, since he struck the negation of the negation from the 'laws' of the dialectic. But to the extent, I say to the extent, that it is possible to abstract from the teleology in the Hegelian conception of history and the dialectic, it is still true that we owe Hegel something which Feuerbach, blinded by his obsession with Man and the Concrete, was absolutely incapable of understanding: the conception of History as a *process*. Indisputably, for it passed into his works, and *Capital* is the evidence, Marx owes Hegel this decisive philosophical category, *process*.

He owes him even more, which Feuerbach was again unable even to suspect. He owes him the concept of a process *without a subject.* It is fashionable in philosophical conversations, which are sometimes turned into books, to say that in Hegel, History is the 'History of the alienation of man'. Whatever the intention behind the pronunciation of such a formulation, it *states* a philosophical proposition which has an implacable meaning, one which is locatable in its offspring, if not discernible in their mother. It is to state: History is *a process of alienation which has a subject,* and that subject is man.

Now, as M. Hyppolite has very well noted, nothing is more foreign to Hegel's thought than this *anthropological* conception of History. For Hegel, History is certainly a process of alienation, but this process does not have Man as its subject. First, in the Hegelian History it is not a matter of Man, but of the Spirit, and if one must *at all costs* (which in respect of a 'subject' is false anyway) have a 'subject' in History, it is the 'nations' that should be discussed, or more accurately (and we are approaching the truth) it is the *moments* of the development of the Idea become Spirit. What does this mean? Something very simple, but if it must be 'interpreted', something important from the theoretical point of view: History is not the alienation of Man, but the alienation of the Spirit, i.e. the ultimate moment of the alienation of the Idea. For Hegel, the process of alienation does not 'begin' with (human) *History*, since History is itself no more than the alienation of Nature, itself the alienation of Logic. Alienation, which is the dialectic (in its final principle the negation of the negation or *Aufhebung*), or to speak more precisely, the *process of alienation,* is not, as a whole current of modern philosophy which 'corrects' and 'contracts' Hegel would have it, peculiar to Human History.

From the point of view of Human History the process of alienation has *always already begun.* That means, if these terms are taken seriously, that, in Hegel, History is thought as a *process* of alienation *without a subject,* or a dialectical process *without a subject.* Once one is prepared to consider just for a moment that the whole Hegelian teleology is contained in the expressions I have just stated, in the categories of alienation, or in what constitutes the master structure of the category of the dialectic (the negation of the negation), and once one accepts, if that is possible, to *abstract* from what represents the teleology in these expressions, then there remains the formulation: history is *a process without a subject*. I think I can affirm: this category of *a process without a subject*, which must of course be torn from the grip of the Hegelian teleology, undoubtedly represents the greatest theoretical debt linking Marx to Hegel.

I well know that, finally, there is in Hegel a *subject* for this process of alienation without a subject. But it is a very strange subject, one on which many important comments would have to be made: this subject is the very *teleology* of the *process*, it is the *Idea*, in the process of self-alienation which constitutes it as the Idea.

This is not an esoteric thesis on Hegel: it can be verified at each instant, i.e. at each 'moment' of the Hegelian process. To say that there is no *subject* to the process of alienation whether in History, in Nature or in Logic, is quite simply to say that one cannot at any 'moment' assign as a subject to the process of alienation any 'subject' whatsoever: neither some being (not even man) nor some nation, nor some 'moment' of the process, neither History, nor Nature, nor Logic.

The only *subject* of the process of alienation is *the process itself in its teleology*. The subject of the process is not even the End of the process itself (a mistake is possible here: does not Hegel say that the Spirit is 'Substance becoming Subject'?), it is the process of alienation as in pursuit of its End, and hence the process of alienation itself as teleological.

Nor is teleological a determination which is added to the process of alienation without a subject *from the outside*. The teleology of the process of alienation is inscribed in black and white in its definition: in the concept of *alienation*, which is the teleology itself *in the process*.

Now perhaps it is here that the strange status of *Logic* in Hegel begins to be clearer. For what is Logic? The science of the Idea, i.e. the exposition of its concept, the *concept of the process of alienation without a subject*, in other words, the concept of the process of self-alienation which, considered in its totality, is nothing but the Idea. Thus conceived, Logic, or the concept of the Idea, is the dialectic, the 'path' of the process as a process, the 'absolute method'. If Logic is nothing but the concept of the Idea (of the process of alienation without a subject), it is then the concept of this strange subject we are looking for. But the fact that this subject is only the concept of the *process of alienation itself*, in other words, this subject is the dialectic, i.e. the very movement of the negation of the negation, reveals the extraordinary paradox of Hegel. The process of alienation without a subject (or the dialectic) is the only subject recognized by Hegel. There is no subject to the process: *it is the process itself which is a subject in so far as it does not have a subject*.

If we want to find what, finally, stands in for 'Subject' in Hegel, it is in the teleological nature of this process, in the *teleological* nature of the dialectic, that it must be sought: the End is already there in the Origin. That is also why there is in Hegel no *origin*, nor (which is never anything but its phenomenon) any beginning. The origin, indispensable to the teleological nature of the process (since it is only the reflection of its End), has to be *denied* from the moment it is *affirmed* for the process of alienation to be a process without a subject. It would take too long to justify this proposition, which I propose simply in order to anticipate later developments: this implacable exigency (to affirm and in the same moment to *deny* the origin) was consciously assumed by Hegel in his theory of the *beginning* of Logic: Being is immediately non-Being. The beginning of the Logic is the theory of the non-primordial nature of the origin. Hegel's Logic is the Origin affirmed-denied: the first form of a concept that Derrida has introduced into philosophical reflection, *erasure (rature)*.

But the Hegelian 'erasure' constituted by the Logic from its first words, is the negation of the negation, dialectical and hence teleological. It is in teleology that there lies the true Hegelian Subject. Take away the teleology, there remains the philosophical category that Marx inherited: the category of a *process without a subject*.

That is Marx's principal *positive* debt to Hegel: the concept of a *process without a subject*.

It underpins *Capital* from beginning to end. Marx was perfectly aware of it. Witness this note added by Marx to the French edition of *Capital*.

Marx: *Le Capital*, tome I (a note found only in the French edition!):

The word 'procès' (process) which expresses *a development considered in the totality of its real conditions* has long been a part of scientific language throughout Europe. In France it was first introduced slightly shamefacedly in its Latin form – *processus*. Then, stripped of this pedantic disguise, it slipped into books on chemistry, physics, physiology, etc., and into a few works of metaphysics. In the end it will obtain a certificate of complete naturalization. Let us note in passing that in ordinary speech the Germans, like the French use the word *Prozess* (*procès*, process) in the legal sense [i.e., trial].[5]

In passing, let me draw attention to the fact that the concept of a process without a subject also underpins the whole of Freud's work.

But to speak of a process without a subject implies that the notion of a subject is an *ideological notion*.

If the following double thesis is taken seriously:

1. the concept process is scientific,

2. the notion subject is ideological, then two consequences follow:

1. a revolution in the sciences: the science of history becomes formally possible,

2. a revolution in philosophy: for all classical philosophy depends on the categories of subject and object (object = a mirror reflection of *subject*).

But this positive heritage is still *formal*. The question posed then is as follows: What are *the conditions of the process* of history?

Here Marx no longer owes anything to Hegel: on the decisive point he contributes something without any precedent, i.e.:

5. Karl Marx, *Le Capital*, t. I (Éditions Sociales, Paris, 1948), p. 181n.

There is no such thing as a process except in relations (*sous des rapports*): the relations of production (to which *Capital* is restricted) and other (political, ideological) relations.

Our meditations on this scientific discovery and its philosophical consequences are not yet over: we are only beginning to suspect them and assess their extent. It hardly need be said that it is not by dabbling in structuralist ideology that we can obtain the means to explore the immense space of the continent that Marx has opened for us (Marx's *Verbindungen* do not amount to a 'combinatory'!).

The continent was opened up a hundred years ago. The only people who have ventured into it are militants of the revolutionary class struggle. To our shame, intellectuals do not even suspect the existence of this continent, except to annex and exploit it as a common colony.

We must recognize and explore this continent, to liberate it of its occupiers. To reach it it is enough to follow those who went before us a hundred years ago: the revolutionary militants of the class struggle. We must learn with them what they already know. On this condition we too shall be able to make discoveries in it, of the kind announced by Marx in 1845: discoveries which help not to 'interpret' the world, but to change it. To change the world is not to explore the moon. It is to make the revolution and build socialism without regressing back to capitalism.

The rest, including the moon, will be given to us in addition.

23 January 1968

Index